How CBS
Tried to Kill
a Book

How CBS Tried to Kill a Book

How CBS
Tried to Kill
a Book

by
Edith Efron
with the assistance of
Clytia Chambers

NASH PUBLISHING, LOS ANGELES

How CBS Tried to Kill a Book

by
Edith Efron
with the assistance of
Clytia Chambers

NASH PUBLISHING, LOS ANGELES

Copyright © 1972 by Edith Efron and Clytia Chambers

All rights reserved. No part of this book may be reproduced in any form or by any means without permission in writing from the publisher.

Library of Congress Catalog Card Number: 72-81830
Standard Book Number: 8402-1280-1

Published simultaneously in the United States and Canada by Nash Publishing Corporation, 9255 Sunset Boulevard, Los Angeles, California 90069.

Printed in the United States of America.

First Printing.

Contents

Preface	ix
Introduction	3
I. Violence	15
"Demonstrators"	16
Black Militants	25
Wallace	41
II. Left	49
III. White Middle Class	67
IV. Conservatives	73
V. War	77
U.S. War Policy	77
Bombing Halt	78
VI. Anti-Nixon Opinion	87
Strongest Anti-Nixon Opinion Excluded	87
Slivers Released to the Press	89
"Safe" Stories Included	98
NBC Joins CBS	114

VII. Democratic Party Dominance	123
Wallace and the Dominant Democrats	123
Nixon and the Missing Republicans	125
Humphrey and the Democratic Alliance	127
VIII. Liberals vs. *The News Twisters*	129
IX. Conclusion	131
Appendixes	137
A. Release by CBS News President Salant	137
B. CBS Study	139
C. "Analysis of Method"	153
D. Winick Study (as summarized by *Broadcasting*)	163
E. UPI Reporter (Tatarian story)	167
F. Testimony of Edith Efron before the Senate Subcommittee on Constitutional Rights, February 2, 1972	171
G. Release on INRA Study	185

Preface

On October 11, 1971, my book, The News Twisters (TNT) was published—a study which reports on the pro and con opinion on a group of controversial subjects transmitted by prime-time network news during the last seven weeks of the presidential campaign of 1968.

In TNT, I conclude, broadly, that in virtually all areas, the elitist-liberal-left line in all controversies was given major play on the air, while the voices speaking for a different view received substantially less coverage or no coverage at all. My most startling findings are these:

- That opinion favoring Republican candidate Richard Nixon had been largely omitted.
- That opinion favoring U.S. government war policies had been largely omitted.
- That opinion was heavily slanted in favor of Black Power separatists and that the views of integrationist Negroes were almost entirely omitted.
- That the networks had dealt with radicals ambiguously—favoring their antiwar, pro-black nationalist positions, but keeping radical leadership virtually off the air.

In sum, TNT *reveals that the conservative, white middle class, moderate Negro, and ideological left groups who had charged network bias against them in 1968 had been justified.*

Before publication, I had sent the TNT manuscript out to about a dozen advance readers chosen by three standards—their distinguished reputations, their scholarship, and their political diversity: Democrat, Republican, liberal, conservative, black and white were approached. The praise was incredibly enthusiastic. Indeed, to quote Dr. William L. Rivers of the Stanford University Communications Department, it was "extravagant"—so "extravagant" that Dr. Rivers was later to write to each of these readers inquiring as to whether they had actually said what the book jacket claimed they had. (They told him they had.)

The book appeared armored with their endorsements under the headline: "Right and Left agree: 'This book is a blockbuster!' "

- A vitally important book about one of the most deadly serious problems confronting America. The author does not present arguments—she presents facts, damning and conclusive. Every citizen should read this book. Nothing more important has been written on why the country is the way it is, in a long, long time.—Allen Drury, Pulitzer Prize-winning author of Advise and Consent.

- A professional tour de force. Edith Efron demonstrates that a public utility has been transformed into a Frankenstein of bias and ideological selectivity of news. Miss Efron's therapy will conceivably unite the broadest coalition of victimized viewers from the New Left to the traditional conservatives. This book is a blockbuster. It should have historic impact.—Murray Baron, cofounder of Americans for Democratic Action and the Liberal Party; former AFL-CIO official.

- Edith Efron has prepared a devastating indictment of network TV news bias. Without an independent investigation of her data and methods, it is impossible to issue a final verdict on her charges. But she has made a *compelling case for a thorough, nonpartisan investigation by Congress of the extent to which the Fairness Doctrine has been evaded by private news managers.—John P. Roche, professor of history, Brandeis University; former assistant to L.B.J.*

● *Fascinating reading—interesting and compelling. I agree with the author's conclusions. I think they are accurate. The description of thirty-three slanting techniques should cause consternation among the self-righteous pundits. But more important, it will better equip the public to scrutinize national news. This book should have great impact on the broadcasting industry. Its publication is a notable event.—Andrew Hatcher, associate White House press secretary to L.B.J. and J.F.K.; black consultant to Kennedy administration on civil rights.*

● *Miss Efron's extraordinary finds are basis for a new ethic in broadcast news. Surely this volume will be the lodestar of reform. Miss Efron is the Ralph Nader of broadcasting, which will never be the same again, and shouldn't.—William F. Buckley, Jr., editor of* National Review; *host of "Firing Line"; ABC guest commentator during the 1968 campaign.*

● *A fantastic, shocking book. It proves beyond any doubt that the networks are politically biased—and that they are lying about it. Even when the slanting is for causes I favor, I find the degree and nature of the bias horrifying. Everyone on the Left should read this book to be properly armed against pseudo-allies. It is a political bombshell.—Dr. George Weinberg, radical writer for the underground press.*

● *The bitter dispute over bias in network television news today is long overdue for an infusion of careful research and non-self-serving analysis. Miss Efron's work is the first serious effort to begin fulfilling this need. Her honest and exhaustively documented study, which indicates a dismal failure by the networks to meet FCC fairness standards in reporting the 1968 presidential campaign, is a goldmine of information and raises dis-*

turbing questions. Some of these bear further study. Others can be answered satisfactorily only by the actions of the FCC or the network newsmen themselves.—Paul H. Weaver, assistant professor of government, Harvard.

• This is a book I wish I had written. It should be required reading for all of the network heads. They would find out what has gone astray in their own shops from the words of their own employees.—Clark Mollenhoff, Pulitzer Prize-winning journalist; former assistant to President Richard M. Nixon.

• Granted that the public media should be free and uncontrolled, we have a right to require that they be fair and responsible. If they are unfair and irresponsible, it makes it difficult to preserve their freedom. Miss Efron's study, based on very impressive documentation, raises this question in an acute and challenging way. It deserves wide and careful attention by all who are interested in public affairs.—Sidney Hook, professor of philosophy, New York University.

Few books in America—and very few politically controversial books—have ever appeared with a phalanx of endorsements from such sharply distinct points on a broad political spectrum. It was powerful evidence that my struggle to present a nonpartisan analysis had been successful.

Indeed, advance reader John P. Roche, professor of history and politics at Brandeis University, wrote in his syndicated column, on July 28, 1971: "[Miss Efron] has provided a prima facie *case of private news management that would bring a true bill from any grand jury in the land.... It might be added that this is not a matter of grinding any special axe—she suggests that the New Left was treated as unfairly as the war in Vietnam!"

On October 11, 1971, a smear campaign of astonishing virulence was officially launched against *The News Twisters*. It was conceived and executed by Richard Salant, CBS News president—a lawyer who was already known to the public as the man who had systematically lied about CBS's dishonest editing practices in the documentary called "The Selling of the Pentagon." The campaign was organized to coincide with the appearance of *TNT* in bookstores across the nation and to influence the first wave of reviews.

Mr. Salant's plan was simple, and—as it seemed to him—unbeatable. A *Variety* reporter named Frank Beerman dug up its major outlines. The story, dated October 6—a week before *TNT* publication—is reproduced here:

CBS ON THE PROWL
vs.
"NEWS TWISTERS"

by

Frank Beermann

The book isn't out yet officially, but Edith Efron's *The News Twisters* is causing all kind of stirs at CBS News. Due in bookstores October 11, it purports to document Miss Efron's charge that all three web news operations favored the presidential candidacy of Hubert H. Humphrey over that of Richard M. Nixon in the seven weeks leading to the 1968 election.

While both ABC and NBC news execs are keeping a low profile on the book, CBS News President Richard Salant has his forces working full steam on refuting the book's material and has even hired two outside research firms to rework the same material.

Miss Efron, a New York staffer for *TV Guide*, examines seven weeks of evening network news scripts from September 16 to Election Day, and uses a word count to "prove" that the webs devoted more talk to pro-Humphrey material than to talk favorable to Nixon.

Under Salant's direction, CBS researchers have already come up with a dossier on Miss Efron and some of her associates in the project. They say they have discovered and are circulating for the eyes of newsmen that the book was financed by a $4,000 grant to Miss Efron in both 1968 and 1969 from the Historical Research Foundation. And although the CBS background material states that neither Miss Efron nor her assistant on the project Clytia Chambers has any identifiable right-wing contacts in their backgrounds, they lean heavily on backing of the foundation by Alfred Kohlberg, late head of the "China Lobby" and its support of a conservative Book Club subsid, Arlington House, publisher of another right-wing attack on broadcasting, "The Left-Leaning Antenna." Miss Efron's book is published by Nash, a Los Angeles firm.

Burning the Midnight Oil

In addition to Salant's pointed direction of CBS's efforts to refute the book, CBS News staff vice-president, David Klinger, and publicity chief Jim Byrne are devoting an estimated one-third of their working days to the effort. Also, archivist Sam Suratt and researcher Warren Mitofsky are spending many hours looking up old scripts and seeking counter-evidence in other CBS shows about the election outside the evening news slot.

The two outside firms hired to assist CBS in its examination of the allegations presented by Miss Efron are International Research Assn., for content analysis, and Mythology, for a word count.

A chief CBS complaint about the book and one which may prove the most profitable to pursue, is the subjectivity laid to Miss Efron in her selection of what is pro and what is anti. CBS claims that any description of President Nixon may wind up in Miss Efron's method as criticism while a Humphrey sketch usually comes out as a favorable comment.

The network is also pointing out that if there is a word-count bias in favor of Humphrey, it is because President Nixon and his advisors chose to keep their campaign under controlled wraps and rarely allowed interviews—while Humphrey and George Wallace both were happy at any opportunity to get mike time.

Total Coverage Missing

CBS says that Miss Efron also misrepresents the fairness doctrine in her focus on one news period. It is their contention that the total election output of the networks, including paid announcements, must be seen as part of the total of presidential campaign material on the air.

CBS, stung as it has been by the critical sniping of Vice-President Spiro Agnew and heavy congressional fire over "The Selling of the Pentagon," would like to convince ABC and NBC that this book is part of the general attack on network news operations. So far there has been little indication that they have set a fire under their colleagues, but in the words of one CBSer, "They'll have to come into this all the way, or we all may wind up castrated news operations."

To translate Mr. Salant's plan: Deciding in advance that *TNT* was part of a large-scale, right-wing administration assault on press freedom, he would (1) issue attacks on *TNT*'s methodology, (2) privately feed *ad hominem* and guilt-by-association attacks to allies in the media, and (3) climax both with documentary evidence that it was a distorted, politically motivated book.

Mr. Salant's operating assumption that there is such a cabal against press freedom is very popular at CBS (as opposed to NBC and ABC[1]). Walter Cronkite has explicitly denounced such a "grand conspiracy." And Frank Stanton, chairman of CBS, has been denouncing "McCarthyism" and implying the existence of conspiracies ever since Vice-President Spiro T. Agnew's speech criticizing network bias in 1969—a speech which voiced the views of some 57 to 70 percent of the population that were already on pollster's records long before he ever became vice-president.

Many in the media view Mr. Stanton as a "statesman" of broadcasting and a hero of liberty for his conspiracy warnings. Others view him as an expert rationalizer who exudes conspiracy charges self-protectively, as a squid exudes ink, every time CBS News is caught in error, distortion or staging of news, which has happened a good deal of late.

The conspiracy theory itself has been actively repudiated by NBC's David Brinkley and by Fred Friendly, former CBS News president, now professor at the Columbia School of Journalism. Mr. Friendly has said that he perceives very little government "meddling in newsroom activities": . . . "The chilling hand that concerns me more is the corporate concern for maximizing profits." Indeed, Mr. Stanton himself has explicitly denied that he believes a conspiracy is afoot—in a context which is worthy of reproduction. Here is the relevant passage of a story from the *New York Times* of October 21, 1971 which appeared under the headline: "Burch, Johnson Deny FCC Interferes With News."

> Mr. Burch [chairman of the FCC] said, "Really I am a bit disgusted that Mr. Stanton keeps bringing up this conspiracy theory, because it won't wash.
> "The theory goes like this. The Vice-President says something, and the FCC will move in and do the dirty work by taking away licences, or whatever. The only thing wrong with the theory is that it's false, and Dr. Stanton knows it's false."
> Dr. Stanton replied to Mr. Burch in a statement this evening.
> "I have never suggested a 'conspiracy' between the Vice-President and the FCC. I have never impugned the integrity of the commissioners.
> "I have said that there is ample evidence of attempts by government officials to intimidate the press. And I have expressed the opinion that *'the whole content and the whole pattern of this government intrusion into the substance and methods of the broadcast press, and indeed of all journalism, have the gravest implications.*'"
> [Emphasis mine.]

I am quite content to believe that Mr. Stanton did not in October, and does not today, believe there is a government conspiracy. He just *implies* it—and permits his chief news star to make the implication explicit. It therefore came quite naturally for Mr. Salant, CBS News president, to invoke the Stanton-Cronkite "conspiracy theory" when *TNT* appeared during this very period. As *Variety* put it on October 6: "CBS, stung as it has been by the critical sniping of Vice-President Agnew and heavy Congressional fire over 'The Selling of the Pentagon,' would like to convince ABC and NBC that this book is part of the general attack on network news operations."

Candidly seeking to project me as part of a government plot to intimidate the free press, and without a stitch of evidence to support such a charge, Mr. Salant set out to trigger a liberal media outburst against *TNT* which would kill it at inception. It apparently never occurred to him that in so doing, *he* was concocting a plot.

The attack on *TNT*'s methodology appeared forthwith—in the form of a brief report by sociologist Charles Winick of CCNY, who was hired by Mr. Salant for the job. Dr. Winick, who has a good scholarly reputation and had no intention of losing it, produced a cautious, heavily qualified and very abstract document.[2] In it, he summed up a series of principles of content analysis which, he said, social scientists considered essential, and he reported that I had not used them. In this, he was correct. *TNT* was based on my own methodology logically derived from a principle of journalism—namely that systematic opinion-loading on one political side of major controversies is an index to the political bias of a news agency. The essence of Dr. Winick's guarded complaint, in effect, was that *TNT*'s methodology was individualistic and non-conventional, which rendered it a barrier to the "credibility" of my findings. At no time did Dr. Winick contest my findings, or a single one of my conclusions. Indeed, Dr. Winick had never laid eyes on my research and textual analyses, and was careful to say so.

Unfortunately for CBS, Dr. Winick did not have a monopoly on what social scientists consider essential or what they find credible. Two social scientists of equal or greater eminence *had* seen my research: they found my new analytical method rationally valid and they supported my work resoundingly.

One was Paul H. Weaver, professor of government at Harvard University, and a media specialist. Professor Weaver had endorsed *TNT* as follows:

> The bitter dispute over bias in network television news today is long overdue for an infusion of careful research and non-self-serving analysis. Miss Efron's work

is the first serious effort to begin fulfilling this need. Her honest and exhaustively documented study, which indicates a dismal failure by the networks to meet FCC fairness standards in reporting the 1968 presidential campaign, is a goldmine of information and raises disturbing questions. Some of these bear further study. Others can be answered satisfactorily only by the actions of the FCC or the network newsmen themselves.

Professor Weaver also appeared publicly as my "witness" on the Public Broadcasting Network program called "The Advocates" (November 2, 1971), where he stated, "I have examined Miss Efron's methodology and findings and satisfied myself that they are substantially competent." And in the Winter issue of the distinguished scholarly journal, *The Public Interest*, Professor Weaver said *TNT* deserved "thoughtful attention," described it as "a serious independent effort . . . [to] . . . shed the light of quantitative evidence on one important aspect of the debate," and said of the analytical method in particular: "Miss Efron's procedure was indeed brilliant in its simplicity." He rebutted criticism of *TNT* methodology as "inconclusive calumny," presented criticisms of his own, and strongly defended *TNT*'s findings on the presidential candidates.

Simultaneously, Dr. George Weinberg's voice was heard. Dr. Weinberg is a psychologist, a research consultant, a mathematician, and author of *Statistics: An Intuitive Approach*, which has been a leading text in American universities for the past decade. Dr. Weinberg issued a statement to the press on October 27. It read:

> I saw Miss Efron's research before reading her book and before knowing her conclusions. I found that my judgments coincided with hers well over 90 percent of the time. The great majority of the statements she classifies as pro or con opinion could hardly be classified otherwise. Miss Efron is far more objective, systematic and explicit in her method than anyone known to me who has ever written a book about TV. After examining her data, I believe that any systematic tabulation by any method would result in essentially the same findings.

And, in a letter written several months later to Dr. William Rivers of the Communications Department of Stanford University, he elaborated:

> Despite many serious differences in political views between Miss Efron and myself, I concur strongly with her conclusions based on the work that she did. Systematic distortion by the major networks, even when it is distortion in the direction I favor, is never satisfactory to me.... Please note that the people who attacked her most loudly did so after declining invitations to see her raw data. What could be lower than that on the scale of human decency?[3]

Others, who like Winick were evaluating *TNT* on its own terms, were also heard from. One was Irving Kristol, Henry Luce Professor of Urban Values at New York University, and co-editor, with Harvard sociologist Daniel Bell, of *The Public Interest*. Mr. Kristol wrote a strongly favorable essay on *The News Twisters* in *Fortune*, November 1971, where he made much the same point as Dr. Weinberg:

> Her research method was simplicity itself.... [It] may seem too simple a methodology, and in an academic sense it is. Were a team of certified sociologists doing this study, on a budget of a million dollars or so, they would employ far more refined and elaborate methods. But it is certain that—on most points if not all—their findings would not significantly differ from Miss Efron's.

And again, another social scientist spoke up—Professor David Ernest Haight of the Political Science Department of Hunter College, CUNY. In the March 1972 issue of *Commentary*, Professor Haight wrote an extensive, scholarly article describing *TNT*'s analytical approach with approval.

> Previous critics have been clearly partisan, apply partisan standards to the coverage given their favorite

topics... Miss Efron has managed to avoid this posture. Instead, in a stroke of rhetorical genius, she has invoked a clearly nonpartisan criterion for network bias.

Professor Haight strongly defended the major findings of *TNT*.[4]

Not all these scholars agreed with my analysis in all respects—some disputing certain interpretations of my data. Nor for that matter did they agree with each other in all respects, a social scientist without a theory of his own being a contradiction in terms. Nor for that matter were they debating Dr. Winick; all, save Professor Haight, had independently evaluated the book before the Winick study appeared. But collectively, their analyses constituted massive support for *The News Twisters*—and an impassable scholarly barrier for Richard Salant.

That has never stopped Mr. Salant, of course, from repeating monotonously that Dr. Winick had "refuted" *TNT*. Five months later, he was still issuing corporate press releases to that effect. Indeed, he has never acknowledged the phenomenon of serious social science support and discussion of *TNT*. It was not civilized, intellectual debate over methods of identifying bias that he had in mind. He wanted only, as *Variety* reported, to convince the media that *TNT* was part of an administration drive to "castrate news operations." And he systematically went about seeking evidence of such a motivation—or, at least, a few facts he could offer the media as apparent evidence. His procedure is faithfully recorded by *Variety* in one paragraph of its remarkable story:

> Under Salant's direction, CBS researchers have already come up with a dossier on Miss Efron and some of her associates in the project. They say they have discovered, and are circulating for the eyes of newsmen, that the book was financed by a $4,000 grant to Miss Efron in both 1968 and 1969 from the Historical Research Foundation. And although the CBS background material states that neither Miss Efron nor her assistant on the project, Clytia Chambers, has any identifiable right-wing contacts in their backgrounds, they lean heavily on backing of the foundation by Alfred Kohlberg, late head of the "China Lobby," and its support of

a conservative Book Club subsid, Arlington House, publisher of another right-wing attack on broadcasting, "The Left-Leaning Antenna." Miss Efron's book is published by Nash, a Los Angeles firm.

My "dossier" was correct in a few respects: (1) I did, gladly, accept a small grant from a conservative foundation to assist me with taping and typing costs—and the book jacket, as well as the acknowledgments, identify it. (2) There are no right-wing contacts in my background or in that of Clytia Chambers. And (3) Nash is my publisher. All true—and a curiously limited "dossier," if I may say so. So limited in fact that it bears detailed examination:

Most curious is the fact that the "dossier" stated what I was *not* politically, but failed to state what I was—a life-long liberal who had evolved, in the face of a cancerous proliferation of state power over the individual, into a libertarian, with no passage whatever through right-wing conduits. Libertarianism is a pro-individualist, anti-statist position that cuts through conventional polarization; it shares certain liberal *and* conservative positions, and opposes certain liberal *and* conservative positions. Depending on any given political situation, one can find libertarians affiliated with either group or with the radical left. The inclusion in Mr. Salant's "dossier" of even a few of my actual anti-statist positions, as they appeared in *Broadcasting* magazine on October 6, 1971—to wit: an opposition to the Vietnam war since its beginning, a fifteen-year-long opposition to the draft—would have revealed that whatever my conflicts with liberalism, I was scarcely a voice of the Nixonian right. That despite my anti-Vietnam position, a conservative foundation should give me a grant for a bias study bespeaks a fairness of mind in projects chairman William F. Buckley, Jr., and a corresponding expectation of fairness in me, which may be ungraspable by Richard Salant. In any event he chose to omit my recorded political positions from his "dossier." They would have demolished his portrait of me as a right-wing stereotype.

Almost equally curious is the way in which Mr. Salant's "dossier" dealt with the question of my publishing house. The "dossier" provided information about a right-wing publishing house, a right-wing book club, and one of their right-wing publications, with which I have had no contact at all. It failed to identify my actual publisher, Nash, a new apolitical house whose authors include CBS star Carol Burnett, Hollywood reporter Rona Barrett, garden expert Jerry Baker, plus a wide variety of liberal, libertarian, and radical writers—the best-selling star of the house being radical ex-priest James Kavanaugh. Nash is also the national distributor for Ramparts Press, a Northern California publisher of radical and radical-left books. Here too the inclusion of such information was clearly inconvenient to Mr. Salant's thesis—so he omitted it. His "dossier" was actually an "anti-dossier": it knocked out everything that might conceivably interfere with his conspiracy theory.

For the rest, this remarkable "dossier" focuses sharp attention on Alfred Kohlberg, the creator of the foundation, not on me. Why the character and values of the original founder are relevant to my book or my motives is not clear to me. Surely, Mr. Salant would not have dreamed of launching a smear campaign on a study conducted with the aid of a similar grant from the Rockefeller Foundation by challenging the probity of its "robber baron" founder or invoking some black militant who had also received a subsidy from that source. Yet that irrelevancy is what he primarily counted on to smear *TNT*—to "prove" it was a distorted vehicle fabricated to destroy freedom of the press.

And he had takers for his shoddy merchandise. *TNT* appeared in October—its birth heralded by a small, shrill chorus of denouncers—all reciting from Mr. Salant's "dossier."

His most agitated outlet was the *St. Louis Post-Dispatch*. On October 6, the *Post-Dispatch* published a news story by its chief Washington correspondent, Richard Dudman. Mr. Dudman obviously thought the dead Mr. Kohlberg the most important aspect of my book. His lead, incredibly, read:

> A new book subsidized by a foundation set up by the late Alfred Kohlberg, leader of the old China Lobby, has touched off a new debate about the objectivity of reporting.
>
> The book is *The News Twisters*, by Edith Efron, a staff writer for *TV Guide*. It was subsidized by the Historical Research Foundation, which was founded with a $175,000 bequest from the estate of Kohlberg, a

wealthy lace importer who supported the cause of Chiang Kai-shek's Nationalist Chinese government in this country for many years.

On October 27, not yet satisfied that St. Louis understood the gravity of the situation, the *Post-Dispatch* followed up with a lead editorial against *TNT:*

> The more we learn of a recently published book, *The News Twisters*... the more it becomes apparent that those doing the twisting are the author and the sponsors of the book.... Actually, the book, employing faulty methodology for the evaluation of the networks' campaign coverage, comes out with conclusions obviously predetermined by its backers' biases.

Why was it so "obvious"? Because, the *Post-Dispatch* told its readers, once again, *TNT* "was subsidized by the Historical Research Foundation, which was founded by the late Alfred Kohlberg"; and Kohlberg, "during his lifetime financed a vast lobbying campaign favoring the Nationalist Chinese and attempting to rescue commercial interests which he had on the China mainland." The immediate editorial conclusion: "The book is no genuine study of TV news performance, but a 1972 campaign document designed to twist network coverage to the right...."

On October 8, Maury Green, TV columnist of the *Los Angeles Times*, declared to his readers that he could tell at a glance, or at least "a second glance," that *The News Twisters* was as phony as "a $3 bill." His climactic reason: the Foundation. "This New York outfit was founded by the later Alfred Kohlberg, a close associate of the late Senator Joseph McCarthy, who crusaded on even shoddier evidence than Miss Efron's."

Also in Los Angeles, on October 1, Dave Kaufman of *Variety* wrote, authoritatively: "*The News Twisters* is a slanted, blatant piece of propaganda..." again citing the Foundation. It was established, he told his readers, by the late Alfred Kohlberg, "who was a close associate of Senator Joe McCarthy, earned the label as 'head' of the so-called China Lobby for his work for Chiang Kai-shek."

On October 4, in New York, Harriet Van Horne, columnist for the *New York Post*, announced to the world that Nash Publishing didn't really exist—at least *she* couldn't find it in a certain directory—and intimated that it was a front organization for William F. Buckley, Jr.

And in the *Washington Post*, on October 11, Ben Bagdikian intoned: "This book . . . deserves examination because it is undoubtedly destined to enter political literature as holy text for those who wish to prove at any price that Spiro Agnew is right." And of course, Mr. Bagdikian, too, climaxed his review with an "expose" of Mr. Buckley and the Foundation—this time, dragging in Louis Budenz.

This outcry against a book, charging "guilt-by-association-with-the-dead"—dead *anti*-Communists, to be sure—is a modern improvement on Joe McCarthy's own technique. It is spectacularly anti-intellectual. But it did not offend the little chorus from the *New York Post*, the *Washington Post*, the *St. Louis Post-Dispatch*, the *Los Angeles Times*. Nor did it offend them while exposing my dead "associations" to suppress all references to the multi-political identity of *TNT*'s living endorsers. All who lift their ideas from those sources are now firmly convinced that *TNT* is a weapon of Nixon-and-the-arch-right-wing, and that I am personally out to "castrate" the free press. That, of course, is exactly what Mr. Salant wants them to think.

What is curious about all this is not the ease with which Richard Salant could trigger a uniform left-liberal howl—or that the howl should come from those particular publications. Nothing is simpler. It is done all the time. No, what is curious is the psychology of the puppet-master, in this case—and his weird indifference to facts: Richard Salant chose a committed defender of the First Amendment to cast as an enemy of the free press!

Item. As a libertarian, I hold the absolutist (or Justice Black) position on the First Amendment, and countenance no government intervention in the press whatever. My position on this issue has been on record for fifteen years.

Item. Richard Salant knows that for years my articles in *TV Guide* have exposed the damage being done to network newscasting by government intervention and regulatory intimidation. I was writing about this long before it was the fashionable thing to do—most notably in series entitled "The Timid Giant" (May 18, 1963) and "Why Speech on Television is not Really Free" (April 11, 1964).

Item. Richard Salant knows that *TNT* itself clearly and explicitly states that I oppose all government regulation of any intellectual, ideological or artistic medium—indeed, that I consider the Fairness Doctrine itself to be a direct contradiction and violation of the First Amendment—the Supreme Court notwithstanding. Richard Salant also knows that a good portion of the broadcast industry was given this information. *Broadcasting* magazine (September 27, 1971) devoted four and a half pages to *The News Twisters*, featuring my position on this issue in a boxed manifesto-like statement in large print. It read:

> The ideal solution is perfectly apparent, although infinitely difficult to achieve after decades of heavily rationalized government intervention into the broadcast medium. It is simply this: to create in broadcasting the identical system that exists in *all other* media of communications in the U.S.—the system which would totally expel government from its confines, and would allow the development of competing news services, each of which had the right to any political point of view if preferred [and which would offer its product] for a fee.... This and only this is the First Amendment system which has given us the incredible wealth of intellectual, ideological and artistic products we have in this country. It stands out in violent contrast to the monotonous, vacuous, ideological-one-note insipidity of standardized network broadcasting. Needless to say, such a reorganization of broadcasting would repudiate the very concept of "public ownership," which is the arch-justification for perpetual government intervention in this medium. It would be a revolution of the broadcast operation down to its very roots.

Item. Richard Salant knows that I stated on the Public Broadcasting Network that I thought the government should be "blown out of broadcasting"; that I have stated it on the "Today" show;

that I have stated it on dozens of local and syndicated shows throughout the country; that I testified to the same effect before the Senate Subcommittee on Constitutional Rights, chaired by Senator Sam Ervin, on February 2, 1972—an appeal for government expulsion that was broadcast live over PBS radio, was covered by the AP, by UPI, by the *Washington Post*, and was printed all over the United States. (My testimony can be found in Appendix F.)

Item. Richard Salant knows that my proposals for government expulsion were discussed *and contested* in the syndicated political columns of conservatives such as Kevin Phillips and Roscoe Drummond—who do not see eye to eye with my libertarian position and are calling (along with many liberals) for tougher regulation of the networks.

To project me as part of a right-wing "plot" to destroy freedom of the press—and to do it continuously and unembarrassedly for almost a year—bespeaks so acute a divorcement from reality that I have frequently worried about Mr. Salant's health.

There is a smear of yet another type for which Mr. Salant is responsible, indirectly, if not directly. In keeping with the fascist/anti-freedom stereotype he has forged for me, Mr. Salant has inevitably generated the rumor that *The News Twisters* is a racist document, and that I myself am a racist. Again, this bespeaks a distressing divorcement from reality.

The News Twisters contains a chapter which exposes the racist stereotypes built into network news—racist sterotypes which were publicly identified and protested in 1968 by such NAACP leaders as Roy Wilkins, Clarence Mitchell and John Morsell. My findings in *TNT* totally document their charges—charges, Mr. Morsell tells me, which persist to this very day. Furthermore, *TNT* was warmly endorsed by Andrew Hatcher. Andrew Hatcher—note it firmly—is a Negro. He said: "I agree with the author's conclusions. I think they are accurate." Mr. Hatcher was, among other things, a consultant to John F. Kennedy on his civil rights policies.

Despite all this, Mr. Salant's attack on *TNT* has generated vicious babble about my "racism." One such response is worth recording. A news photograph was circulated by UPI which is almost uniquely venomous. It is a picture of George Wallace, holding up *The News Twisters* with a satisfied grin on his face. The UPI caption cites from the book—but somehow it fails to mention the fact that *TNT* describes Mr. Wallace as a representative of the "racist right" (page 60). It also, somehow, fails to mention the fact that *TNT* charges the networks with forging racist stereotypes or that *TNT* is supported by distinguished black civil rights leaders.

The timing of UPI's release of this photograph is of interest. It was sent out on November 9, a week and a half after UPI editor Roger Tatarian denounced *The News Twisters* as a distorted study—a conclusion reached, he said, after an "independent check." His "independent check"—which will be discussed later, along with the equally "independent checks" of the other critics already quoted—is lifted right out of a CBS document. On the basis of CBS' priming of Mr. Tatarian, and of Mr. Tatarian's attack on *TNT*, UPI decided to circulate a photograph, nationwide, whose tacit yet palpable message was: *The News Twisters* is racist.

This alone suffices to reveal the gutter level of the campaign triggered by Mr. Salant. But it does not reveal it completely. Mr. Salant knew a few other facts which are mysteriously missing fron his "dossier" on me which he handed out to his media outlets. They were presented in clear English, in unblurred print, in the publicity bio which accompanied *The News Twisters* on publication. The facts: My former husband is a Haitian. I have a mixed-race son. Further: I am the author of studies and monographs on the Afro-French culture of the Antilles. And my associate Clytia Chambers earned her Master's degree at Howard University where she worked under Dr. E. Franklin Frazier, the noted Negro sociologist. When Mr. Salant privately talked his media friends into attacking *TNT* as the voice of American reaction, he did not tell them this. And so much for the crudest applications of the CBS conspiracy theory.

I arrive now at the most complex of Mr. Salant's enterprises: his determination to offer "documented evidence" of the alleged fraudulence of *TNT* data—evidence he required to back up his propaganda.

Deriving the "evidence" was a complex enterprise for a very simple reason: there wasn't any. He could hunt for minute errors—

and did. He could bicker over details—and did. But he could not shoot down the most politically explosive findings—and never has. It is of interest to point out here that if indeed I had manufactured such data in *TNT*, it would have been child's play to demonstrate. *TNT* is full of extreme and specific charges, and nothing could have been easier to knock down, had those charges been false.

Example. I stated in *TNT*, and testified before Senator Ervin's subcommittee (see Appendix F) that the bias against candidate Richard Nixon in 1968 was almost entirely dependent upon the *absence* of pro-Nixon opinion—a crucial shortage of Republican and pro-Republican sources of opinion.

In the case of CBS, in particular, I declared that only on four days during the seven campaign weeks studied, did CBS carry any opinion from the American public and that only on one day, October 28, did CBS carry any opinion from Republican sources in support of Nixon.

What could be easier than to give me the lie—if it had been a lie? All Mr. Salant would have to do would be to flash the examples I had overlooked on the screen or publish them in the press. He never did it.

Example. I stated in *TNT*, and testified before Senator Ervin's Sub-committee, that the bias against President Johnson's war policy was almost entirely dependent upon the *absence* of pro-war opinion.

In the case of CBS in particular, I declared that only on one day, October 9, did CBS carry any such opinion—from President Johnson himself.

What again could be easier than to prove me wrong—if I had been wrong? Mr. Salant merely had to publish the examples of opinion favoring Mr. Johnson's war policies which I had suppressed. He never did it.

And again, if I am fabricating when I charge that virtually no opinion was heard from moderate, anti-violence, pro-integrationist Negroes, what could be easier for Mr. Salant than to name the ones I left out? He never did it.

Mr. Salant's research team did "burn the midnight oil," as *Variety* put it. It burned for six weeks. And yet to this day of writing—nine months after that team began its work—no refutation of the major findings of *TNT* has ever appeared.

Mr. Salant did invest a small fortune in a *pretense* at refuting those findings, and thereby hangs a tale:

Among his most publicized actions was the commissioning of an independent research firm—International Research Associates, of New York City—to review the entire period of CBS coverage dealt with by *TNT*.

In October, *Broadcasting* reported that this super-scientific study was due shortly. Then again in November, various voices in the press assured us that it was due shortly. And again, it was due shortly—in December, in January, in February and in March. Something extraordinary was holding it up. But what?

More than five months after the controversy over *TNT* had exploded—long after it had passed the point of paroxysm—CBS News quietly sent out a press release announcing that the INRA study was ready (Appendix G). Its headline read: "Second Independent Study Refutes Bias Charge." Its lead announced that INRA had reported "findings radically different from the claims made by Edith Efron in her book, *The News Twisters.*" And then it announced its most significant news:

> Using established content analysis techniques accepted by the social science research community, INRA found that while Miss Efron had reported 16 times greater anti-Nixon material than pro-Nixon material in the 36 broadcasts during the 1968 presidential election campaign, the breakdown of all references to the presidential candidates indicated 62 percent of the Nixon material to be neutral, 19 percent judged favorable to him and 19 percent unfavorable.

The clearcut implication: I had committed dire errors or had fabricated most of the anti-Nixon findings.

Those, however, are the findings Professor Weaver of the Harvard University Department of Government discusses most extensively in his study in *The Public Interest*. And one of the things he said was this: ". . . my own inspection of two different samples of Miss Efron's file of anti-Nixon opinion convinces me that, by any reasonable standard, the large majority of such items are in fact quite clearly anti-Nixon opinion; no more than 20 or 30 percent of the anti-Nixon items might be questioned."

Dr. Weinberg had also seen the data, and he agreed with some 90 percent of the classifications.

Surely, we did not, all three, share the same political bias: By self-description, Professor Weaver is a centrist, Dr. Weinberg is a radical leftist, and I am a libertarian. A more politically varied "jury" could not exist. What's more, Professor Weaver and Dr. Weinberg had never met or exchanged opinions. Had we all been hallucinating?

The very next paragraph of the CBS news release was even more puzzling, if possible. INRA, according to CBS, had reported a greater amount of "material" favorable to Humphrey than to Nixon: 26 percent vs. 19 percent. This painful admission was accompanied by a small torrent of explanations to the effect that Humphrey spoke favorably "of himself" more often than did Nixon.

There was something bizarrely vague about all this terminology—and this relaying of percentages with no reference to totals. What, I wondered, was "material"? And what were its measurable attributes? In *TNT*, I use a word-count method to quantify, and the word is the basic unit of measurement. What basic unit was INRA using? The release did not say.

I obtained the original INRA research, and discovered to my astonishment that for these findings, INRA was using, as its basic unit, the *paragraph*. Discreetly embedded within the study, on page 34, was this information:

	NIXON %	HUMPHREY %
Favorable	19	26
Neutral or balanced	62	57
Unfavorable	19	17
Total number of paragraphs	(382)	(402)

How long were those paragraphs? Two sentences? Five? Half a page? The INRA study does not say. There is no way on earth to compare the amounts of favorable and unfavorable "material" involved.

And what does it mean to compare the Humphrey-Nixon percentages if their bases are different—402 paragraphs of unknown length vs. 382 paragraphs of unknown length?

And can INRA paragraphs of unspecified length be compared with word-count findings in TNT? Of course not.

INRA refused to reduce its paragraph units to a common denominator of word counts, and I know exactly why:

CBS, in 1968, gave significantly more coverage to Humphrey's statements than to Nixon's—a fact confirmed in the *Variety* story (page 13). Indeed, at the annual meeting of the Philadelphia Society held in October at the Sheraton Hilton Hotel in New York City, Russ Bensley, executive producer of the show, "CBS Evening News with Walter Cronkite," admitted this before about four hundred people. This imbalance between Humphrey and Nixon coverage was a desperate worry of Richard Salant who kept seeking to rationalize it without ever naming it. Thus, in one of the earliest documents issued by CBS on *TNT* (Appendix C), he offered five "hypothetical" reasons for which a news service *might* cover the speeches of one candidate more than another—the identical theoretical discussion in which INRA later engages (INRA Introduction, pages iii and iv). Curiously, these "hypotheses" were never connected to the actual transcripts, but they constitute the conceptual glue which holds the INRA findings together.

INRA did not reduce its vague percentage-of-paragraph findings to word counts for good reason: to camouflage the disparity between the Nixon-Humphrey totals. But the imbalance in coverage was so striking that even the camouflage failed: Humphrey still came out with significantly more favorable "material."

There was one other set of INRA findings that was of inestimable importance. INRA had also been obliged to report a striking pattern of shortage of Republican sources as opposed to Democrat. Specifically, INRA reported (INRA, pp. 8, 13, 26): a shortage of Republican party figures as opposed to Democrats (11 percent to 46 percent); a shortage of references to the Republican party as compared to the Democratic party (8 percent to 16 percent); a shortage of Republican "people or groups" as compared to Democrats (3 percent to 16 percent); and a shortage of "public officials favorable to Republicans" as opposed to Democrats (8 percent to 20 percent).

But those were the only possible sources of pro-Nixon opinion! The arch-basis for my claim of anti-Nixon bias—clearly offered in *TNT* and presented as evidence before the Ervin hearings—was a shortage of Republican and pro-Republican sources. INRA had, even by its own CBS-protective methodology, supported my most politically explosive findings.[5]

The original INRA research, indeed, turned out to be a veritable gold mine. Although repeatedly arguing on the basis of CBS-provided "hypotheses" that its findings did not necessarily prove bias, INRA was broadly supportive of *TNT* in three major areas, all identified as "Highlights" of the study: (1) CBS coverage contained more favorable material on Humphrey than on Nixon (INRA "Highlights," page xii). (2) CBS coverage contained more favorable material on Muskie than on Agnew (page xii). (3) CBS coverage revealed a shortage of Republican sources (page x). In other words, the *trends* of the INRA data and of *TNT* data were identical: they were pro-Democrat.

All this, of course, was rigorously excluded from the CBS press release. CBS News President Richard Salant counted—correctly—on the mental inertia of the hand-out broadcast press to use his official version of the INRA findings. Thus, the *Daily Variety* headline of March 13, 1972: "Efron Book's Bias Charge Shot Down"—with the CBS release printed intact.

There are other elements in this singularly dishonest press release and in the INRA study which I have not discussed (i.e., CBS's pretense that INRA's study was a replication of *TNT*'s analysis; INRA's failure to cover the other issues in *TNT*). This suffices, however, to establish that Richard Salant's only real purpose in commissioning and publicizing the study was to declare *TNT* "refuted," to portray CBS News as exquisitely fair to candidate Richard Nixon—and to provide "evidence" that I had fabricated my Nixon data as part of a broad administration assault on the free press. He had systematically laid the groundwork for this; a lawyer, he had prepared his case.

But his case backfired. There was too much, even in the commissioned INRA apologetics, that was embarrassingly congenial to *TNT* findings. So Mr. Salant took his time about announcing the study. By the time he sent out his intensely selective press release, few, if any, in the general media were interested. To this day, almost no one in the country has ever heard of the INRA study, so loudly heralded by Mr. Salant at the time of *TNT*'s publication, as the forthcoming "scientific proof" that *TNT*'s bias charges were false.

In the last analysis, Mr. Salant has never counted on the social sciences to come to his rescue. He had not counted on Dr. Winick and he had not counted on INRA. Even the most cooperative social scientists, anxious for good consultants' fees, have a reputation to protect. They simply could not provide the service Mr. Salant required—either to wipe out the full reality of the biased CBS transcripts—or to provide documented proof that *TNT*'s data were politically motivated.

That service could only be supplied by Mr. Salant himself and the group of men working under his direction, of whom one of the most important was a man named James Byrne. Mr. Byrne is not known for his particular competence in the field of content analysis. He is a public relations executive, i.e., a hired CBS propagandist, attached to the CBS News department.

The Salant-Byrne team, with its eye firmly on public relations, produced a ten-page study which, unlike the commissioned professional studies, was stuffed with comparisons between CBS transcripts and *TNT* texts. This study of *TNT* was, from the beginning, and remains until today, the chief weapon in Mr. Salant's arsenal and the only one he had ever counted on to accomplish his goals. Preface apart, this book is a detailed analysis of that study and of the means used by the CBS team to "prove" *TNT*'s alleged distortion.

Technically this book is part of my testimony before the Ervin Subcommittee. In my oral presentation, I discussed it briefly—and I here quote the relevant section:

> Omission—the crudest slanting technique in the journalistic repertoire—is the principal technique in network slanting. It is perhaps inevitable therefore that when CBS chose to attack *The News Twisters*, its attack was a monument to this very slanting technique.
>
> In September, before *The News Twisters* was published, a ten-page document was distributed to the

nation's media by CBS. The mailing literally blanketed the country. It is a study of *The News Twisters* conducted by the CBS News Department itself. It claimed to present hard, documentary evidence of the degree to which I had grossly distorted CBS transcripts. This evidence, said CBS, was based on a "spot check" of those transcripts.

That document is a fraud. Its fraudulence consists in a systematic omission of every conceivable piece of information either from CBS transcripts or from *The News Twisters*' text which would make my classifications intelligible and would reveal the reasoning behind them. The effect of these omissions was to make my work seem arbitrary, irrational and dishonest.

Seventeen charges were listed by CBS—a number that is statistically insignificant for my study, although CBS did not mention this fact to its readers—and of these seventeen charges, fifteen contained active misrepresentations of either CBS transcripts or *The News Twisters*' text or both. I have prepared a detailed report for the Committee in which I identify every misrepresentation; restore every violated context; present the stories that CBS sought to conceal; and I have identified the precise principles by which CBS conducted its so-called random "spot check." My analysis reveals that it was not a "spot check" at all but a carefully calculated smear planned to discredit my book before publication. I call this report "How CBS Tried to Kill a Book."

The remarkable CBS "study" served to provide "facts" to confirm the Salant conspiracy-interpretation of *TNT*—"facts" which clearly implied willful distortion of the CBS data and outright fabrication of findings. It served as a bible for the critics in the press. The widest use of it was made by those critics already cited. Some, like Ben Bagdikian and Harriet Van Horne, and later, Roger Tatarian, UPI editor, quoted from it extensively and blindly. Others used it to a lesser degree and as background material. Virtually all embroidered the results with compatible charges of their own.

Here is a chart listing some of their assessments of *TNT;* the CBS misrepresentations they used as "evidence" for their attacks; and the sections of this book where those misrepresentations are analyzed:

CRITICS' ASSESSMENT	CRITICS' ATTACKS DRAWN FROM CBS "STUDY"6	PAGES WHERE CBS MISREPRESENTATIONS ARE ANALYZED
". . . right-angled paranoia." Harriet Van Horne *New York Post* October 4, 1971	"Some examples of [Miss Efron's] documentary proof: . . .	
	"[Her charts show that] CBS broadcast 2388 words in favor of Hubert Humphrey . . . slightly more than the 2083 words spoken against Humphrey. CBS therefore—as any first-grade mathematician can see—is biased against Richard Nixon. . . .	page 127 (Chapter VII, Democratic Party Dominance)
	"[S]he came up with astonishing figures. On ABC, she writes, reporters 'sanctioned violence eleven times.' On CBS, nine times and on NBC seventeen times. At no point does she define 'sanctioned.' Is acknowledgment that a riot took place 'sanctioning' it? . . .	pages 15-48 (Chapter I, Violence)
	"During the campaign, CBS had a film clip of Vice President Humphrey saying, 'The Rap Browns, the Stokely Carmichaels, the extremists of the left and the right will not have their way, and we will not allow them to terrorize or stampede America. . . .'	pages 73-75 (Chapter IV, Conservatives)

"Miss Efron calls these remarks 'anti-conservative.' Her comment on that broadcast (text supplied by Mr. Salant) is: 'Humphrey attacks extremists of the right for violence. 9/16/68.' In her judgment, extreme rightists and conservatives are the same. Interesting."

". . . dishonest, inaccurate . . . demonstration on how to doctor evidence."
Ben Bagdikian
Washington Post
October 11, 1971

"Networks biased in favor of liberals? On page 40 she has a graph labeled, 'The number of words spoken for and against liberals on the three networks combined—ABC, 77 for, 112 against; CBS, 0 for, 120 against; NBC, 101 for, 474 against.' By my calculations that makes network words 20 percent for liberals and 80 percent against liberals. By Miss Efron's it comes out network bias in favor of liberals. . . .

page 129
(Chapter VIII, Liberals)

"The pro-Humphrey bias? One of the more intriguing studies in human emotion will be the look on Hubert Humphrey's face when he reads on page 50 that in the 1968 campaign the media treated him as a 'quasi-saint.' But that would be unscientific. . . .

page 127
(Chapter VII, Democratic Party Dominance)

"On page 330 Miss Efron says that the CBS newscast of September 30 is an 'editorial' in which a 'reporter supports demonstrators.' According to CBS, the actual broadcast transcript says that Humphrey 'has not, however, figured out how to handle the demonstrators.

pages 17-20
(Chapter I, Violence)

PREFACE xxxvii

When the hecklers wish, they can dominate his campaign appearances, and that frustrates and angers Humphrey and his staff. To that extent, at least, the hecklers have the upper hand.' That's what the author calls 'reporter supports demonstrators.'

"She lists as an anti-Nixon 'editorial' a passage she paraphrases as 'says Nixon is overconfident; suggests he is a liar.' The CBS script: 'Nixon says he is warning his staff against overconfidence, but he himself hardly looks worried.'"   pages 105-109 (Chapter VI, Anti-Nixon)

"Miss Efron proves that she herself excels at [twisting facts]."
Roger Tatarian, vice-president and editor
United Press International
October 28, 1971

"For example, on page 281, she writes that on September 25, 1968, a CBS reporter 'says Nixon has a rancorous streak; says Nixon is overconfident; suggests he is a liar.'   pages 105-109 (Chapter VI, Anti-Nixon)

"If this is what the CBS reporter said, Miss Efron's charge of bias is proved. But when you get the actual text from CBS, you find that what the reporter said was: 'This week's tour, all in friendly territory, is to reassure the faithful, and to boost local GOP candidates. Nixon says he is warning his staff against overconfidence, but he himself hardly looks worried.'

"Again, on page 312, Miss Efron lists a CBS broadcast of September 25, 1968, in which, in her words, 'Reporter attacks   pages 67-71 (Chapter III, White Middle Class)

> white middle class as racists.' According to CBS, the precise words which Miss Efron interpreted in this manner were: 'From Pennsylvania, Muskie flew to Michigan and there in Taylor, a white middle class suburb of Detroit, was heckled by supporters of George Wallace. Correspondent Herman reports he handled them with as much aplomb as he handled college hecklers.' "[7]

In every case, these are serious misrepresentations. The famous CBS "study" of *TNT* was a public relations operation from start to finish. It was geared to feed small publishable nuggets of distorted or actively falsified material into the media and to pull them out again as authoritative "press opinion" on *TNT*.

On October 13, a brief two days after the publication date of *TNT*, CBS mailed out the earliest feedback from its own mimeograph machines: the cooperative reviews from Bagdikian, Van Horne, etc.—and sent them to all its own affiliates. The accompanying memo by John A. Schneider of CBS was directed to "Officers and Department Heads of CBS, Groups, Divisions and Subsidiaries." It said:

> On September 29, I forwarded to you Dick Salant's statement on Edith Efron's *The News Twisters*. Dick's views are shared by highly qualified critics, as *you will* note from the attached reviews. [Emphasis mine.]

They were "shared" indeed.

The public relations machinery worked efficiently, giving CBS material from "qualified critics" to send out in infinite streams whenever the disturbing question of *TNT* came up. It succeeded in killing planned stories in *Newsweek* and *Time*. It worked just as "Dick" thought it would work—with one small hitch.

Not everyone, even those confused and puzzled by the superficial cleverness of the CBS study, was a blind believer. Not everyone was an automaton who could be triggered to reflexive denunciations with cue words and unsubstantiated conspiracy theories. And not everyone swallowed down whole self-serving CBS "studies" prepared by a CBS lawyer and a CBS public relations executive.

At the height of the attack came a new wave of endorsements, again from people of varied political persuasions—again of intellectual and professional distinction. Here are the statements used in an ad for *TNT* which appeared in the *New York Times* on December 7, 1971—two months after the Salant campaign was launched; to wit:

"*The News Twisters* deserves to be read, not just read about."—Roscoe Drummond, the *Christian Science Monitor*.

"No one who reads Miss Efron's book will ever listen again to TV network reporters with the same ears as before. . . . Miss Efron is a remarkably astute and well-informed lady. . . . It would take a combination lawyer, philosopher, political scientist and sociologist to deal effectively in a review with all the fine points she raises in her tightly reasoned book. . . . She also writes clearly and well so that someone who is schooled in none of the above disciplines can see the relevance and importance of her analyses and the questions they raise. . . . This book deserves wide and serious attention. Perhaps it's my 'liberal bias' that makes me think it will get it."— Katherine Gauss Jackson, ex-Contributing Editor and reviewer, *Harper's Magazine*; Board of Trustees, Freedom House; in *Freedom at Issue*.

"An impressive statistical case which cannot be dismissed with mere general denials."—Arthur Krock, former Chief, Washington, D.C., Bureau of *The New York Times*.

"We have long needed a systematic and non-impressionistic survey of this whole troublesome area (of ideological bias in television newscasting), and now we have one ... Edith Efron takes good aim and scores many direct hits. ... The techniques of biased reportage are various, and Miss Efron discusses them in a shrewd and insightful way."—Irving Kristol, *Fortune* Magazine.

"The electronic propagandists who run U.S. network television are currently staggering and reeling under their most devastating blow. ... Edith Efron has written a book that may just infringe on the patent for TNT."—Kevin Phillips, syndicated political columnist, author of "The Emerging Republican Majority."

"*The News Twisters* is must reading for everyone concerned with news—those who write, read, direct, view or listen."—Steve McCormick, Vice-President and News Director, Mutual Broadcasting, Washington, D.C.

"*The News Twisters* is like a necessary breath of fresh air to an industry which has been perhaps overly self-protective. I find *The News Twisters* in total agreement with my own experience in the industry."—Ted Kavenau, Vice-President and News Director, Metromedia Television, New York City.

"TNT aptly describes this book's explosive potential ... the book provokes thought. [Miss Efron's] solutions to the problems she perceives ... deserve consideration. ... The book is a hot item if the early reaction is any indication. It is must reading regardless of whether one agrees with Miss Efron's position."—*The Quill*, Journal for Professional Newsmen.

"Here is a book that should be read by every voter of whatever political conviction, by every high school and college student, by every viewer of TV network news. It should be distributed by book clubs and condensed in *Reader's Digest*. Most of all, it should be read carefully by the Federal Communications Commission."— S. I. Hayakawa, President of San Francisco State College, in the *Los Angeles Herald-Examiner*.

And hundreds of invitations to appear on television and radio shows; hundreds of reviews, columns, news stories, editorials poured in from every point in the nation—the overwhelming majority of them fair and favorable. As usual, the rest of America did not react as did the "New York-Washington axis."

Indeed, many of those who had received the CBS "proof" of my alleged turpitude dismissed it or debated it. Again, to cite people of significantly different political persuasions (and only material that appeared in print):

In his essay in *Public Interest*, Professor Weaver demolished the entire CBS study in a few phrases. He pointed out that "CBS, prior to the official publication date, issued a long memorandum 'refuting' Miss Efron's content analysis using two dozen examples" and he dismissed them as "too few to be statistically capable of confirming or falsifying the study."

Dr. Weinberg blasted off against those who issued studies of *TNT* without having examined my raw data and analyses (*Variety*, October 27): "To dispute findings without close scrutiny of the author's data is intellectually dishonest. The act of releasing studies of someone's research without examining that research is indefensible."

West Coast syndicated TV columnist Ernie Kreiling (December 2, 3); San Francisco State College President S. I. Hayakawa in the third of his October series of columns on *TNT;* and political columnist Roscoe Drummond, in a *Christian Science Monitor* review of *TNT*, October 21, actively contested the CBS material.

And on March 6, editor Robert Bleiberg of *Barron's Weekly* wrote a full-page editorial on the CBS executives' "contempt for truth" in both controversies over "The Selling of the Pentagon" and *The News Twisters.*

The complex PR operation, intended to kill *TNT*, didn't kill it. Politically paranoid, dishonest and out of contact with reality, it backfired.

On December 13, two months after Richard Salant's campaign hit high gear, *TNT* hit *Time*'s best-seller list.

Two months later, I was invited to testify on my findings and solutions before Sam Ervin's Senate subcommittee, and had an opportunity to present my charges of fraud against CBS in one of the most important forums in the land. Inevitably, my testimony was blacked out by the networks. But it was carried live by Public

Broadcasting Radio Network, was beamed throughout the country—and created a demand for my analysis of the CBS study, which follows.

Unlike this preface, it is not a fairly fast-paced tale of a High Noon clash between two sides, before which one can remain a relaxed spectator. It is a slow-paced review of a set of 1968 news stories, contrasting my actual analyses with Mr. Salant's version of my analyses; it requires concentration and personal effort on the part of the reader.

But the ultimate meaning of both this preface and the study that follows is the same: Both are exposés of guilt.

Guiltless men do not imagine a cop behind every bush. Guiltless men don't pretend that a libertarian journalist who is well known to them has suddenly been transmuted into an agent of repression. Guiltless men don't smear, don't use ad hominem attacks, don't slander, don't use guilt-by-association techniques, don't feed misleading "dossiers" and false information to the press. Guiltless men don't seek to destroy professional reputations in the face of a purely intellectual challenge. Guiltless men don't misrepresent the results of professional studies—and labor for six weeks with public relations men to create phony ones.

If you read the following analysis of CBS's public relations study of *TNT* slowly, carefully and in its entirety, you will learn more than you can imagine about the mental processes of the executives in those CBS News offices as they checked their own broadcasts against *TNT*'s charges. You will learn exactly what they feel so guilty about; why so many groups in America are antagonized by them; why every strong challenge to their fairness scares them into fits; and why a pioneer bias study was such a threat to them that they had to cry conspiracy in order to deal with it.

You will learn not only *how* but *why* CBS tried to kill a book.

EDITH EFRON
New York City

May 1972

[1] NBC has never publicly contested *The News Twisters*, choosing silence as its official policy. ABC, embarrassed by the fact that its chief commentator, Howard K. Smith, is on record with a bias analysis similar to mine, and that it no longer has the tapes of the 1968 period, prefers to engage in discreet correspondence.

[2] For an accurate summary of Dr. Winick's major criticisms which appeared in *Broadcasting* magazine, see Appendix D. Those who wish to read it in its entirety are advised to write to CBS News and request a copy.

[3] Quoted by Dr. William Rivers, at the Journalism Convention sponsored by The Charles Edison Memorial Youth Fund in New York City, February 13, 1972, and recorded in its published transcript.

[4] Further discussion of Professor Haight's study can be found on page 4.

[5] See page 126 for an indication of how INRA discovered so much "material" favorable to Nixon, despite this extreme shortage of Republican and pro-Republican sources.

[6] The CBS "study" in its original form is to be found in Appendix B.

[7] See pages 114-120 for NBC's contribution to Mr. Tatarian's list, which compounded the CBS misrepresentations.

How CBS Tried to Kill a Book

Introduction

It is customary when charged publicly and unjustly with a series of wrong actions to defend oneself first against the gravest of charges. For example, if one were unjustly accused of chronic duplicity, of being irritatingly late to appointments, of faulty grammar, and of nail-biting, one would, rationally, attend first to the charge of chronic duplicity, second to the charge of lateness, and one might never even get around to the less significant charges.

A rational man would not rush into a room, hastily pin these four charges on a dart board, blindfold himself, and hurl a dart randomly at the charges—resolving to answer whichever one the dart landed on. Obviously, the dart might land on the nail-biting charge—and he would not have cleared himself of the charge of chronic duplicity.

In other words, a rational man does not deal with a group of accusations leveled against him—accusations ranging from scandalous to minute—by a random "spot check" method. He defends himself systematically against the worst charges.

CBS News considers the charges in *TNT* of such importance that it feels compelled to defend itself in a nationwide campaign. Yet CBS News announced to the country that it had chosen to defend itself by a random "spot check" method.

I have analyzed CBS' "spot check" method in detail as it culminated in the CBS study—and hereby report on its curious nature:

Bulk of Findings Omitted

CBS's random "spot check" did not land on the bedrock of *TNT*'s documentation—that huge mass of pro and con opinion from candidates, politicians, organizational and institutional leaders, private citizens, and foreign statesmen, which constituted the bulk of *TNT*'s findings. This body of opinion is explicit, undisguised, consisting of overt, intelligible approval or disapproval, endorsement or repudiation, of the presidential candidates, the war, the U.S. bombing in Vietnam, etc. Both the patterns of this opinion and most of the specifics are a matter of historical record. George Ball did endorse Humphrey, the AFL-CIO leadership did denounce Wallace, "demonstrators" did oppose the war, etc.

The mass of overt, readily identifiable opinion is the unshakable foundation on which *TNT* stands. It has been disputed by no one. It constitutes 82 percent of the opinion transmitted by NBC, 69 percent of the opinion transmitted by CBS and 51 percent of the opinion transmitted by ABC, on the issues studied. This non-editorial opinion is the actual fountainhead of network bias.

TNT makes this clear in the fifth chapter, "The Parallel Principle" (page 123), and a related Appendix O. That chapter and its appendix demonstrate that if *only* this body of overt, undisguised opinion is considered—omitting all reference to reportorial opinion—the bias results are preponderantly liberal-left in type. To cite a few quantitative examples from CBS News alone: With all reportorial opinion omitted, the mass of opinion on Nixon carried by CBS is nine to one against him; almost two to one against the U.S. policy on the Vietnam war; six to one against the U.S. bombing halt policy; three to one in favor of the left, etc.

In *Commentary*, March 1972, Professor David Haight of the Political Science Department of Hunter College, CUNY, bases his entire support of *TNT* on this rockbed of opinion. He points out that no charges of error have been directed against my coding of "interviews, excerpts from speeches, and so forth," and writes:

INTRODUCTION 5

Network news contains a large proportion of such direct quotations from partisan sources and coding *them* is simple. A child could identify the bias in Eugene McCarthy's comments on Richard Nixon or U Thant's view of America's Vietnam policies; establishing a panel to do so is like establishing a panel to determine whether the speakers are male or female. When such material is separated from the reporters' comments—and Miss Efron does separate it, in one of her chapters and in one of her numerous appendices—the pattern remains evident in nearly every topic. . . .

Neither the networks nor [antagonistic] reviewers have commented on this aspect of the book. Unless they can show that Miss Efron simply added wrongly, it is hard to see how they *could* comment.

CBS's random "spot check" never hit this unshakable base of opinion save for two items, and CBS misrepresents both of them. Both illustrations consequently are worth identifying here:

1. The first is analyzed on page 73 of this report. It is a short opinion by Hubert Humphrey, aired on 9/16, which denounces three different groups: black militants and extremists of the left and right. CBS criticized *TNT*'s classification of this material, severely misrepresenting the classification method and portraying it as evidence of political bias in *TNT*. The reader is requested to turn immediately to page 73 for a detailed explanation of the misrepresentation involved.

2. The second example does not appear in the CBS study, and consequently is not analyzed later in this report. It appears in a corollary document (Appendix C) but because it is the only other example from this base-opinion that CBS has ever mentioned, and because it is also misrepresented, I analyze it here.

It is a CBS story, 10/15, on an anti-Wallace demonstration by hippie "hecklers," as the CBS reporter names them, who usually follow Wallace in droves, baiting and booing him, and whom he customarily denounces. On this single occasion, the hecklers decided to "rattle Wallace" by cheering and shouting "We want Wallace!" rather than jeering him. CBS cites this as a characteristic example of the inordinate difficulty of classifying opinion pro or con.

CBS then challenges *TNT*'s classification of this expression of public opinion as anti-Wallace opinion. CBS quotes its own reporter's story as saying, "It was bound to happen. The hippies, those whom George Wallace calls anarchists, decided to come to one of his rallies and put on a different kind of show." And CBS declares that these two particular statements were the basis of *TNT*'s classification of this public opinion as "anti-Wallace," adding, "Clearly, this is a subjective evaluation."

That, however, was *not* the basis of *TNT*'s classification. It is just the lead of the story, and does not report on opinion at all.

CBS leaves out the rest of the story. It fails to explain how the CBS reporter knew that these were "hecklers," i.e., hostile to Wallace; how the CBS reporter knew that Wallace was hostile to them ("You boys had better have your say because after November 5, you're through in this country."); and why the CBS reporter concluded: "It was comical for a while, but (. . .) it hit on the edge of smiling violence." In other words, CBS omits from its story precisely those sections in which the CBS reporter makes it quite clear that this was an anti-Wallace demonstration. It cuts out the sections on which *TNT*'s classification was actually based.

There was no ambiguity about this situation in the least. Three networks reported on it identically. NBC writes: "The protesters tried a reverse psychology. Several hundred of them, many dressed in hippie garb, cheered and hollered, and went wild at everything Wallace said. . . . But they would not let him speak and the tactic was devastating. Wallace himself got angry and flustered." And ABC had a similar report.

It is unquestionable that three individual reporters of three networks perceived that this was a unique anti-Wallace protest in an ironic form, and stated so. *TNT* simply reproduced the *network* classification.

On this ludicrous basis, and by means of citing an atypical example and chopping out all relevant portions of a CBS text, does CBS charge me with making "clearly subjective" estimates and *TNT* with faulty classifications.

INTRODUCTION 7

The two above items—their pettiness transcended only by CBS's equivocation—are the *only* challenges that CBS has ever made to the bulk of opinion material on which *TNT* rests.

Worst Inequities Omitted

In addition, the random "spot check" vaulted right over the most blatant inequities revealed by *TNT* for the seven-week period studied:

NUMBER OF WORDS OF OPINION

Against Nixon	5300	vs.	320	for Nixon
Against U.S. war policy	651	vs.	287	for U.S. war policy
Against U.S. bombing halt policy	407	vs.	36	for U.S. bombing halt policy
Against the white middle class	258	vs.	0	for the white middle class
For black militants	1578	vs.	742	against black militants
Against conservatives	84	vs.	0	for conservatives

AND

For Humphrey	2388	vs.	320	for Nixon
Against Nixon	5300	vs.	2083	against Humphrey

The CBS "spot check" study did not mention or contest one of these relationships, the nuclear revelations of political bias.

Patterns of Evasion Omitted

The CBS "spot check" leaped right over *TNT*'s additional charges that whole classes of opinion categories were omitted from network coverage in areas where they were clearly relevant: opinion from moderate civil rights leaders; opinion from right-of-center opponents of the war; opinion from middle-class, pro-law-and-order blacks; opinion from liberal critics of New Left totalitarianism, etc. Only one such charge was touched on by CBS's "spot check"—an area in which CBS found one word error in *TNT*—which it brandished in bald-faced misrepresentation of the magnitude of the charge itself. (See pages 51-59 for a full explanation.)

Similarly, the CBS "spot check" assiduously ignored any charge of omission of politically significant single stories which had appeared on one or both of the other networks—such as J. Edgar Hoover's warning to the nation, on 10/1, of present and imminent New Left violence. The "spot check" did alight on one such charge where *TNT* had erroneously omitted one CBS opinion. (See page 59.)

Apparently, the random "spot check" chose to acknowledge this category of evasion charges only where error could be cited in *TNT*.

Harshest Political Charges Omitted

Again, the CBS "spot check" flew birdlike over a variety of interpretive political charges pertaining to Democratic Party dominance of coverage patterns. Instead, it alighted on fragments of phrases which it wrenched out of their qualitative context, presented them as though they were quantitative statements and then "rebutted" them with *TNT* statistics on other findings, charging *TNT* with self-contradiction. (See pages 124, 127.)

No such serious charges of political partisanship were ever acknowledged by the CBS study, let alone disproved.

Explicit Editorial Opinion Omitted

When it came to the far smaller category of reportorial opinion, the "spot check" again had its own special radar. It avoided all consideration of explicit editorial opinion. It never happened to encounter Eric Sevareid when he came out from behind his veiled profundities, when he described the United States as "one of the world's mightiest powers bombing and smashing one of the world's weakest" (10/22), or when he said, "It is deeply unsettling to see Richard Nixon, unyoung, unhandsome, unsexy, adored by female teenagers. . . ." (9/17).

Selected: "Safe" Stories

The "spot check" then hovered over one aspect of network-engendered opinion—that of implicit editorial opinion—exercising busy selectivity:

- It omitted all stories where the covert opinion was so strong that the implications could be seen by the untutored eye.
- It seized upon innocuous splinters from some of these stories—individual sentences—releasing them to the press as evidence of the innocence of those stories (and of the corresponding distortion in *TNT*) but omitting them from the study.
- It selected for the final study stories, or sections of stories, which appeared politically safe, even innocuous.

Texts Manipulated

Within this "safe" category, the "spot check" frequently manipulated CBS transcripts; it

- Omitted significant sections which had served as the base for *TNT* classification.
- Presented sections which had not served as the base for *TNT* classifications.
- Rewrote two sections, omitting crucial contexts for *TNT* classifications.
- And even appears to have changed one text retroactively, the better to contest a *TNT* classification.

TNT Analyses Omitted

The "spot check" finally explored the dangerous terrain in *TNT*, where implicit editorial opinion was analyzed and summarized—both within the text, and as one-line statements in the appendix. And, rapidly, it knocked out the following crucial information:

- It omitted the fact that *TNT*'s one-line summaries were presented as the sole practical means of offering the reader "a bird's-eye view" of seven weeks of opinion—explicit and implicit.
- It omitted the fact that behind all one-line summaries of implicit editorial opinion stood *TNT* research—available for inspection, and containing lengthy textual analyses of every implicit editorial opinion that had appeared on the air in seven weeks.
- It omitted the fact that the one-line summaries of implicit editorial opinion were distillations of these lengthy analyses—translated into overt language. *TNT* explains this translation system clearly:

"In the case of all opinion save editorial, the original opinion was explicit. In the case of editorial opinion, the original may have been explicit, implicit, or a combination of both; *the condensation process itself renders all explicit.*" (*TNT*, page 257.)

- It omitted the more extensive summaries—which elaborated on the covert meaning of this same editorial opinion—that appeared elsewhere in the book.
- Finally, it omitted all the Slanting Techniques summaries—summaries which explained the technical means by which the reporters communicated this covert meaning.

In other words: CBS' random "spot check" operated on *TNT* like a laser beam—delicately excising the whole dimension of implicit or covert opinion as though it did not exist and was not relevant to the stories the "spot check" had chosen for the study.

And it then presented *TNT*'s one-line distillations of such implicit opinion as if they were literal descriptions of the *overt* text, and declared:

In story after story, there is just no resemblance between the story as broadcast and Miss Efron's description of that story. They simply do not state what Miss Efron claims they state.[1]

The CBS Study

The study, which was the direct result of this "random" investigation, was ten pages long. In its final form, it included this curious assortment of "charges" against *TNT:*

> nine charges of distorted content analysis—five of them misrepresenting CBS transcripts and *TNT* texts, four of them misrepresenting *TNT* texts alone
>
> five fabricated contradictions between *TNT* conclusions and *TNT* statistics—four of the five based on misrepresentations of *TNT* text and one an irrelevancy
>
> one complaint over a classification heading, accompanied by misrepresentation of *TNT* text
>
> one word error, accompanied by misrepresentation of *TNT* text
>
> one missing opinion.

In addition, there were a few other charges of transcription errors mentioned on the side, e.g., "dissident" instead of "dissenter," "censure" instead of "censor," etc.

Finally, the entire study was presented as though it were exclusively a compendium of content-analysis charges, although there were only nine.[2] The opening of the CBS study said:

> CBS News has made a "spot check" for the purpose of this Appendix of the transcripts of CBS News broadcasts listed by Miss Efron in support of her conclusions. The pertinent portion of each broadcast has been identified—and the actual broadcast text, Miss Efron's description of that text and her pro or anti classification are quoted. These few examples, among many which can be cited are a measure of the accuracy and fairness of her facts and conclusions.

Thus, the CBS "spot check" study was sent out across the United States before the publication date of *TNT*, October 11, 1971, to fulfill its appointed mission—that of destroying *TNT* at birth.

It is quite apparent, of course, that CBS did not conduct a "spot check" at all. No random investigation—even assuming a random investigation to be rational—pursues so purposeful a course. No random investigation could—without Divine intervention—so successfully steer away from the immovable bulk of basic charges, from the most catastrophic instances of unfairness, from the most important revelations of evasion, from the most serious political charges, from the most blatant examples of reportorial bias. No random investigation could, time after time, spot a fragment of a qualitative evaluation which could be made to sound quantitative if torn out of context. No random investigation could evade every reference to implication, covert opinion, slanting methods and techniques—while landing only on the most heavily camouflaged and subtle examples of implicit opinion.

No random investigation—indeed, not even random stupidity or random malice—could result in misrepresentation in fifteen of the seventeen charges against *TNT* in a ten-page study.

Why was it necessary for CBS to describe this as a "spot check" when it so blatantly is not? The answer is quite clear:

If the CBS "finds" are pulled out at random, the assumption of their applicability to the totality of *TNT* is credible. The very "randomness" permits CBS News President Richard Salant to pen this sweeping charge: "There is one basic flaw which permeates and completely discredits the book . . . in story after story, there is just no resemblance between the story as broadcast and Miss Efron's description of that story. . . ."

Further, if the CBS "finds" are pulled out at random, the impression is created that there has been no screening out of incriminating material. By a "random" method, CBS would be as vulnerable to exposure as *TNT*.

In other words, it was necessary for CBS to claim that it was using a "spot check" to communicate the impression of honesty—and avoid being charged with systematically forging a smear.

But that is precisely what CBS has forged.

In the chapters that follow, I break the CBS examples down into categories, under the subject headings in *TNT* to which they are applicable. This act of classification alone is illuminating: it allows one to see that the authors of the CBS study carefully selected certain examples from each category, and equally carefully left out others—for self-protective reasons. The CBS study, in its original form (Appendix B), looks like a chaotic compendium of random examples. It was planned to look that way. My orderly organization of these examples tells a very different story.

The organization of the chapters themselves moves from the simplest and grossest distortions by CBS to the progressively more subtle and complex. Thus, while you might be more interested in a subject that appears later on in the book—such as the treatment of the presidential candidates—you are advised to read the material in the order presented. As you read, you will become gradually familiar with the basic types of misrepresentations involved and CBS's repertory of techniques; this will prepare you for the more complex examples.

In certain chapters, I present additional material not referred to directly by CBS at all. This is always to demonstrate CBS's selectivity—what it chose to leave out.

You will note that I quote from *TNT* at regular intervals—and in a few places, extensively. At no time is the *TNT* material intended to serve as a rebuttal; that would be circular reasoning. It is there only to show the context that CBS has violated.

As I said earlier, the chief slanting technique of network journalism is the technique of *omission*. Over and over again, you will see that when these omissions are rectified, when the missing material is put back into place—my statements and analyses become fully intelligible. You may not *agree* with some of my textual analyses in their complete presentation. That is your privilege. But even in disagreement, you will perceive that they are not *arbitrary*, they are *reasoned*—they emerge from the facts in full context.

A few words, here, about my textual analyses of covert editorial opinion might be helpful. Almost invariably, I analyze by reference to the slanting technique of omission. The primary question I pose to each story is: *Was there an important alternative interpretation of this subject which could logically have been present but was not?* The missing alternatives are almost always opinions or assessments which prevailed in the center-to-right band of the spectrum of opinion from blacks and whites.

That does *not* imply that I think each story should necessarily have included those alternative views. It implies only that they were not present. The method is required in order to arrive at a final tabulation. For example: if, out of twenty stories on a controversy, Side X is presented, and Side Y is missing from each, one can proclaim the coverage biased against Side Y. But one would not know this unless *each* story had been tested for the presence or absence of *both* sides.

With these few tips, you are now ready to read. If you have never seen the CBS study, I advise you to turn to Appendix B and to read it through immediately in its original form, remembering: that is the document that was mailed to the U.S. media *before TNT* came out.

---

[1] CBS News President Richard Salant, Press Release, accompanying the CBS study, October 11, 1971. (See Appendix A.)

[2] Out of a total of 300,000 words analyzed for *TNT*, nine disagreements on classification (even free of misrepresentation) are negligible. CBS would have to challenge 30 to 40 percent of the total findings to question the thesis of the book.

I. Violence

TNT reports that network stories have been found which contain reportorial rationalization of or evasions of political violence.

TNT also reports that these editorial rationalizations of violence took several standardized—and invariably tacit—forms:

- The reporter glamorized an advocate or practitioner of violence, thus enhancing the advocacy or practice itself.
- The reporter minimized or evaded the advocacy or practice of violence while covering the advocate or practitioner, thus whitewashing or glamorizing him.
- The reporter criticized or undercut critics of violence and law-and-order advocates, implicitly supporting the objects of their criticism.

On this subject, the CBS study says:

Miss Efron's book contains many sweeping, highly accusatory pronouncements, supported by little or no evidence or only by tortured rationalization. These extreme statements, which hardly read like scholarly conclusions by an objective analyst, provide insight into Miss Efron's own biases. This is one example:

On ABC, reporters sanctioned violence eleven times; on CBS, nine times; and on NBC, seventeen times. In Appendix N a complete list of all references to the stories containing this opinion will be found. This quiet, steady spewing-out of justifications for violence by allegedly responsible men, under the eyes and ears of allegedly responsible network management, is a pathological phenomenon. [Page 95.]

And CBS concludes (italics mine):

These are strong words. *But an inspection of the transcripts of the nine CBS news broadcasts cited by Miss Efron shows no justification whatsoever for such charges.*

In other words: CBS is flatly claiming that no CBS reporter, during the period of the study, ever favored an advocate or practitioner of violence . . . ever minimized or evaded the issue of violence while covering an advocate or practitioner . . . ever criticized or undercut critics of violence and law-and-order advocates . . . and that no trace of such implications is to be found in the nine stories cited by *TNT*.

CBS's claim is false.

In this chapter, all nine stories will be presented, and *TNT*'s charges will be fully documented.

The chapter is divided into sections called "Demonstrators," "Black Militants" and "Wallace"—the categories in which CBS violence-sanctioning has been found. Each section will also contain a description of the additional misrepresentations by means of which CBS sought to reinforce its claim that there is "no justification whatsoever for such charges."

"Demonstrators"[1]

CBS carries two stories which contain implicit editorial opinion sanctioning "demonstrators'" violence.

VIOLENCE

Story Number One

This story is referred to on the first page of the CBS study itself (Appendix B, page 140). It is the major example of news distortion uncovered by *TNT*, as well as an illustration of covert editorial support of violent "demonstrators."

Here is how CBS chooses to present it; the CBS study says:

> *9/30/68 CBS News Transcript:* After broadcasting an excerpt from a Humphrey campaign speech, CBS News reported that Mr. Humphrey "has not, however, figured out how to handle the demonstrators. When the hecklers wish, they can dominate his campaign appearances, and that frustrates and angers Humphrey and his staff. To that extent, at least, the hecklers have the upper hand."
>
> *Appendix K (page 330):* Miss Efron classifies this report as a "pro-demonstrator editorial" by the reporter and comments: "Reporter supports demonstrators (demonstrators politically unidentified)."

This presentation of *TNT*'s analytical process is fraudulent:

- CBS chops out half the reportorial narrative upon which the pro-"demonstrators" classification was based.
- CBS chops out the "excerpt from a Humphrey campaign speech," although the content of this excerpt is central to the charge that the CBS reporter tacitly sanctioned "demonstrators' " violence.
- CBS chops out a crucial addition to *TNT*'s statement as it appears in Appendix K, page 330. This statement is followed by a footnote, giving further information on this story. It reads: *"Editorial rationalization of violence;* for summaries, see Chapter III, section on 'Demonstrators'."
- CBS omits all reference to the indicated summary, which describes the editorial rationalizations of violence in detail (page 80).

18   HOW CBS TRIED TO KILL A BOOK

TNT SUMMARY
   Here is the summary that CBS omitted:

> *9/30:* The CBS reporter completely suppresses the Humphrey attack on the totalitarian and Hitlerian conduct of those who threaten violence and propose to tear down this society—an attack culminating in Humphrey's statement that no democracy should stand for this. This story was carried on both ABC (9/30/2, Anti-"Demonstrators") and NBC (9/30/2, Anti-"Demonstrators"). Instead, the CBS reporter quotes Humphrey as sanctioning dissent and portrays him as though he were endorsing those whom he criticized so violently. This wiping out of an attack constitutes support of those attacked.

CBS BROADCAST[2]
   Here is the actual section of the story on which *TNT* charges are based (the reportorial narrative alone is italicized):

> **Reporter:** *The demonstrators, although they are a small minority, Humphrey claims, are constantly on his mind. Even in the Mormon Tabernacle with the nearest heckler hundreds of miles away, he could not forget them.*
>
> **Humphrey:** Now my ears echo with the voices of dissent. Yet I stand before you to confirm this above all: I believe in the right to be different, the right of dissent, not for some but for everyone. America in a sense is built on dissent. As the (. . .) of this valley surely know, dissent is the dynamo of democracy, in Utah as in all America. When the people of the nation can move their heads in one direction only, up and down, they must soon bow them down forever.
>
> **Reporter:** *Humphrey can handle the truth squad, Nixon and the press. He has now to figure out how to handle the demonstrators. When the hecklers wish, they*

> can dominate his campaign appearances, and that frustrates and angers Humphrey and his staff. To that extent, at least, the hecklers have the upper hand.

TEXTUAL ANALYSIS[3]

The significance of this entire story lies in what the CBS reporter suppressed—and in the implication of this suppression.

What was suppressed was the major theme and content of Humphrey's speech. Both NBC and ABC report that the major theme of this speech was an attack on violent "demonstrators."

According to NBC-TV, Humphrey said:

> They would destroy homes and businesses and lives in their supposed zeal to correct injustices. And you know and I know that they must be stopped. . . . And they are of no one ideology, but they all share a basic disdain, yes, a hatred for the democratic processes and democracy itself. They say they propose to tear this society down and build a new one on its ashes—and I quote them. They have tried to shout down presidential candidates, and they say they will disrupt the polling places on Election Day. [See NBC 9/30/3—Anti-"Demonstrators."]

According to ABC-TV, Humphrey also said:

> They are those who are preaching the same order of doctrine of disorder and anarchy, and they're using totalitarian tactics in the street—the very tactics that brought dictatorship to Europe, that brought Hitler to power. . . . They have tried to shout down presidential candidates, and they say they will disrupt the polling places on Election Day. They even threaten to break up the inaugural ceremony next January 20th. And in the meantime, they promise, in their language, 50, 100, 200 more Chicagos. Ladies and Gentlemen, my fellow Americans, no democracy can, nor should any democracy stand for it. [See ABC 9/30/2—anti-"Demonstrators."]

The CBS reporter, however, suppresses this. Instead, he mocks Humphrey as being unreasonably obsessed with the demonstrators: They "are constantly on his mind"; and, even "with the nearest heckler hundreds of miles away, he could not forget them." In sum: The reporter criticizes Humphrey for what is "on his mind," while keeping the content of Humphrey's speech secret from the CBS viewer.

When the reporter does quote Humphrey on the violent "demonstrators," he selects a passage which presents Humphrey's belief in the right to dissent. This creates the illusion that Humphrey was defending the violent "demonstrators," when instead he was denying that the First Amendment protected their conduct. The reporter is making it seem that Humphrey is morally sanctioning the "demonstrators," when he attacked them strongly.

The distortion is compounded by the reporter's conclusion. He describes Humphrey as helpless before the "hecklers," who "have the upper hand." But Humphrey's speech actually conveyed scorn and contempt for the violent "demonstrators": He was looking *down* on them. The reporter is distorting the *moral* relationship between Humphrey and those he condemned as "Hitler jugend."

In summary: This reporter has grossly manipulated and distorted the facts in order to portray Humphrey as passive and impotent before the violent "demonstrators." This is why the editorial narrative is classified both as pro-"demonstrators" and anti-Humphrey.

It is also why *TNT* cites it as an illustration of a story in which the reporter tacitly sanctions "demonstrators' " violence: He has suppressed a powerful attack on their violence, and mocks and undercuts the man who engages in this attack.[4]

Story Number Two (Excluded from the CBS Study)

In 1968, a widespread charge by the liberal and left world was that "law and order" was code language for racist repression—that all who were opposed to political violence and riots were racists. This charge against opponents of political violence was itself a tacit sanctioning of that violence. In the CBS story that follows, one long section tacitly communicates this point of view.

VIOLENCE

TNT SUMMARY

Here is the summary of that report as it appears in *TNT* (pages 80-81):

> *9/30:* The reporter justifies violence by attacking the American middle class which opposes "violent dissent" and "student riots." He says they are "white"—suggesting a racist motive—and that they are intellectually "limited." He describes the demand for "an end to violence" as a "Wallace theme"—i.e., a racist theme. This assault on the middle-class opposition to "student" violence and riots is a defense of violence and riots.

CBS BROADCAST

Here is the section of the CBS story on which this analysis is based. It is the latter half of a long story on Agnew and the "white middle class" (only relevant reportorial narrative is italicized):

> **Reporter:** ... *And throughout the campaign, Agnew has hit many of the Wallace themes—the need for an end to violence (...) an end to student riots, urban (...), and the need, in short, for law and order.*
>
> **Agnew:** A report recently released by that great American J. Edgar Hoover, and I'm proud to call (...) indicates that serious crimes have increased 57 percent in the last seven years, that two-thirds of all the crimes of violence committed are by young people under the age of twenty-one years. It tells me that the permissiveness that prevails in our society, that is encouraged by those who rationalize and excuse lawlessness of any form—who allow any form of dissent as long as the so-called objective is meritorious—is tearing down America today.
>
> **Reporter:** Agnew, not Nixon, has drawn the heaviest Democratic fire. . . .
>
> **Humphrey:** Nixon has already made his first appointment, Spiro T. Agnew. Now listen to what the *Washing-*

ton Post said: "Mr. Nixon's decision to name Agnew as his running mate may come to be regarded as perhaps the most expensive political appointment since the Roman Emperor Caligula named his horse to the Council." Now, I want you to think as I say: "President Agnew."

Reporter: How do you feel about yourself? Your qualifications?

Agnew: I think I qualify. I have a capacity, in my judgment, to make a decision and (. . .) intelligence and ability to perform the office. I have successfully performed in the governorship. I think my presence on the government relations committee has given me a voice that has been respected and listened to on the national scene.

Reporter: Agnew's strength as a campaigner lies not in (. . .) of new ideas. *It lies in the (. . .) of middle-class whites. I like him, they murmur during the rally. I like what he says. They react because he is one of them, the kind of man who might be and was president of the local PTA. He shares their worries about what is happening to the white middle class, their fears of crime, of violent dissent and* of militant class (. . .) *He shares their limitations too, their short horizons.* Agnew critics say that Agnew's strength as a campaigner is also his weakness as a vice-presidential candidate, as a man who could be president of the United States.

TEXTUAL ANALYSIS

In this section of the story, the reporter engages in systematic undercutting of the anti-violence viewpoint both in Agnew and in the "white" middle class:

• The reporter describes Agnew as hitting "Wallace themes" while campaigning. These "Wallace themes" are defined as: "the need for an end to student riots," and "the need, in short, for law and order."

To refer to such positions as "Wallace themes" is tacitly to suggest that their sole motive is racist, that only racists feel the "need for an end to violence" and to "student riots." This is a severe undercutting of the anti-violence position.

• Having implicitly linked Agnew's anti-violence position to racism, the reporter then lets Agnew speak on this subject directly. Agnew expresses concern over growing crime and violence and attacks those who "rationalize and excuse lawlessness in any form."

• The reporter follows this immediately with a report on Democratic criticism of Agnew, featuring a film clip in which Humphrey compares Agnew to Caligula's horse. The placement of this unusually strong attack necessarily undercuts the views Agnew was expressing and expresses thereafter: Once again, this is a severe undercutting of his anti-violence position—additionally implying that it is a position held by the stupid.

• In the final wrap-up of the entire story, the reporter reinforces both implications—of racism and stupidity:

He switches to Agnew's supporters, and describes them as the "white" middle class, implying that these supporters are reacting to Agnew in terms of their color, or race prejudice. Thus, he reinforces his earlier implication of racist motivation for the anti-violence position.

• He then talks with condescension about their fear of "crime," and of "violent dissent," as if these were things only inferiors feared. And he makes his condescension explicit: He describes the "limitations" and "short horizons" they allegedly share with Agnew.

This consolidates the editorial message that only racists with intellectual "limitations" and "short horizons" are disturbed by "violence," by "violent dissent," and "student riots."

This is a final severe undercutting of the anti-violence position and of those who hold it, and the entire story ends on this note.

• This story was classified as pro-"demonstrators," and as an illustration of tacit editorial sanctioning of political violence, by means of systematic undercutting and criticism of those who are opposed to it.[5]

How the CBS Study Deals with "Demonstrators"

To understand how CBS chooses to deal with *TNT*'s "demonstrators" findings, which include two significant examples of covert reportorial sympathy to violent "demonstrators," one must see them as part of a particular context in *TNT*.

TNT sums up the opinion pattern on "demonstrators" as follows, on page 83:

> In terms of total word counts, opinion on "demonstrators" is a paradox. Both on ABC and CBS, anti-"demonstrator" opinion substantially outweighs pro-"demonstrator" opinion. Only NBC conforms to the dominant pattern.
>
> These statistics, however, give only partial information. They do not reveal the fact that an internal "debate" of a systematic kind is going on between editorial opinion and "establishment" opinion.
>
> On all three networks, the leaders of this country repeatedly charged the demonstrators with criminal lawlessness. But reporters on all three networks have either: no criticisms . . . or petty criticisms . . . or cloak the misdeeds with protective euphemisms . . . or actively rationalize their commission . . . or pretend there is no issue of criminal lawlessness at all.
>
> This is so massive an editorial undercutting of the serious charges as to render the statistics unreliable as guides.

The CBS study seeks systematically to obliterate *TNT*'s report on this complex pattern of coverage—without acknowledging its existence or answering the question it raises. It does so by two means:

1) It cites only one story (Number One) in this category ostensibly as an illustration of *TNT*'s alleged dis-

tortions. The CBS misrepresentations in this story have already been described in detail.

2) The CBS study also issues the following accusation:

Miss Efron includes an extended discussion aimed at showing that the networks favored "demonstrators" (pages 76-83). Yet her word count (page 45) shows that CBS was against demonstrators, 1304 to 609.

This is active falsification of *TNT*'s analysis and conclusions as quoted above. The "extended discussion" was *not* "aimed at showing" that the networks favored "demonstrators." It was "aimed at showing" that while the word totals were anti-"demonstrators," an internal "debate" existed, with "establishment leaders" consistently on the anti-violence side, and network reporters consistently on the pro-violence side.

CBS falsifies this *TNT* text and cites *TNT* statistics in spurious opposition, for the obvious purpose of generating a charge of self-contradiction in *TNT*.[6]

Black Militants

In this section, I present four stories—all of which were classified in *TNT* as containing editorial opinion that was pro-black militant. In all four, the reportorial narrative also served as a vehicle for the tacit sanctioning of violence.

Each story is prefaced with the summary of this editorial opinion as it appeared in *TNT*. And each is followed by a textual analysis.

Story Number One (Excluded from the CBS Study)

TNT SUMMARY

10/24: The reporter glamorizes a black-power athlete who is threatening to burn cities. He repeatedly calls him a "hero," omits existing black criticism of his conduct, portrays him as the voice of a monolithic black community (*TNT* page 71).

CBS BROADCAST
   (The reportorial narrative which contains the opinion is italicized.)

   Reporter: Last week American Negro athletes, Tommy Smith and John Carlos, won medals at the 200 meter dash at the Olympic games in Mexico City. As they stood on victory podiums during the playing of the Star Spangled Banner, they raised their arms in the symbolic black-power salute. *With black-power spokesmen H. Rap Brown and Stokely Carmichael, John Carlos received a hero's welcome as he began a national speaking tour.*

   Carlos: Too many white people telling me I was a fool and saying that Tommy Smith and I were wrong and I was very honored and pleased to come home to the black community and find (. . .)

   Reporter: *After Carmichael and Brown, the black community had two new folk heroes in their two athletes.*

   Black militant: Now anything I want to say to the black athletes who participated in those games illegally is that I wish you fourteen years of leg trouble.

   Carlos: All we want to say is that we don't want to have a big speech. We want to let the United States of America, we want to let the whole world know, that we are going to pick our heroes from today on.

   Reporter: *Carlos, who offered his bronze Olympic medal to a museum for black people, showed himself to be a bitter hero.*

   Carlos: I didn't believe in it, but I stood up anyway because I didn't want no static, but those days are gone. You'll never see me stand up, tell this thing, that national anthem represents me. I want you to know another thing. The United States booed and harassed Tommy Smith and myself, and I think we did it the best way we could possibly do it. If there ain't no change (. . .) we're really going to be running around a flaming city.

Reporter: *Later Carlos received the admiration of students at Howard University. They joined him in the now famous gesture of defiance.*

TEXTUAL ANALYSIS

This story is about athlete John Carlos, expelled with athlete Tommy Smith from the Olympics after they conducted a black-power demonstration during the playing of the U.S. national anthem. In this story, Carlos issues a political threat before a black-power audience: *"If there ain't no change (. . .) we're really going to be running around a flaming city."*

The CBS reporter converts this entire news story into problack-power propaganda, thus sanctioning this threat of setting a city aflame. He does this by several means:

- Carlos states that "white people" said he and Smith were "wrong" at the Olympics, and that "the black community" honors him for his action. The CBS reporter does not see fit to correct this statement. *The facts:* Carlos and Smith were also criticized by black athletes at the Olympics, who did not share their demonstration, and who disapproved of their action. ABC-TV carried interviews with such black opposition on October 18. By failing to elaborate on black opposition, the reporter supports Carlos' inaccurate claim to be monolithically endorsed by "the black community."
- The reporter further reinforces this claim by repeating Carlos's actual words, and presenting them as fact. He, too, states that "the black community" supports Carlos. But the reporter does not know what all American blacks think about this issue. He is engaging, here, in collective "mind-reading," and transmitting an unjustifiable over-generalization about the black com-

munity. This, too, has the effect of aggrandizing Carlos (and the other black power advocates), and converting them into black heroes, adulated by all blacks.

- This is actually the only editorial purpose of the story—a purpose so crudely handled that it is blatant. The reporter's *only* narrative content is a contrapuntal beat of "hero"—"hero"—"hero." In the lead, he describes "a hero's welcome." In his first transition, he described these "new folk heroes." In his second transition, he calls Carlos a "bitter hero." In his conclusion, he transmits the acclaim of Howard University students (implying all of them).

Apart from this insistent proclamation of Carlos's "heroism" in the black community's "mind," the reporter has literally nothing else to say. There is no other editorial information in the story, and critical views have been screened out. The reporter is simply functioning as a human echo chamber for the cheers of black-power advocates.

It is in the context of this editorial lionization that Carlos's threat to set a city aflame is set like a political jewel. The lionization of an advocate of violence constitutes tacit sanctioning of that advocacy.

Story Number Two (Excluded from the CBS Study)

This is a more complex, and more covert story, in which the reporter uses a variety of slanting techniques to communicate his tacit sympathy for black rioters.

TNT SUMMARY

    9/26: The reporter rationalizes a violent black-power riot in a Boston school in which twenty people were injured by euphemistically calling it "unrest" and by equating it to an expression of black "pride" and black "identity" (*TNT*, page 71).

CBS BROADCAST

(The reportorial narrative which contains the opinions is italicized.)

Reporter: This is one evidence of the protest, a black power meeting yesterday in a Boston park.... The Negroes had demanded a student union in one high school and the right to wear dashikies and African pull-over shirts to class. *To some this may seem a minor matter, but to Negro militants here, it is part and parcel of their demands for more black influence in schools.* State representative Michael Haynes endorsed the demand for African dress.

Haynes: Well, I don't see why anyone should make such a to-do over a dashiki. Well, the dashiki is just a garb that somebody is wearing.

Reporter: *The protest had spilled into the streets. Several hundred protestors were confronted by police in blue uniforms and police recruits in khaki. Stones and bottles were thrown, windows were broken. There was trouble elsewhere in the city. All together twenty persons injured. One person dead from a heart attack. The demonstrators in turn charged police brutality. Eventually the unrest died down....*

School-Committee Chairman: It is important to note that a very revealing statement was made by Mr. (...) who is a resident of Newton, a former teacher with the famous Meadowbrook School, now the vice-principal of the so-called Liberation School in Boston, that it was his intention and the intention of those he purportedly represents to overthrow the school committee and the school system and dictate policy (...). This is really the root of it.

Reporter: *... And for many of those who came to school today, there was some sense of wonder at it all.*

Black student: They talk about our dashikies, and the hippies, they go to that school, all sorts of people (with) beads and all that.

Reporter: *This dispute, then, is a commentary on the civil rights agony of Americans and how far it has moved in the course of the last decade. But this dispute has nothing to do at all with integration. White and Negro students go to school together here in Boston. But what is at stake is a matter of black identity, black pride, and how the Negro students choose to express it.*

TEXTUAL ANALYSIS

The reporter's narrative sections of this story are a vehicle for both covert and overt rationalizations of a violent black-power riot in a Boston school.

- The reporter opens the story with an ostensible report on clashing opinions over the rioters' demands to wear dashikies to school. "Some," says the reporter, consider this a "minor matter" on which the school should not be intransigent, and he shortly quotes a politician to that effect: "It's just a garb." "But to Negro militants," says the reporter, it's a way of gaining black "influence" over the school.
- This is a perfect "Some-say-this, but-others-say-that" structure, appropriate for presenting two sides of a debate. But it is a contrived distinction. It presents only one side of the debate: The reporter paraphrases the black rioters, and the politician speaks on their behalf.
- The missing half of the debate does not show up until about two-thirds of the way through the story. The school committee chairman declares that it's not just clothes which generated the riot—that it was inspired by a black-militant group which wants to take over the school and dictate policy.
- By disintegrating this debate, and offering a mock substitute for it in the introduction, the reporter is initially presenting the conflict in terms exclusively favorable to the rioters.
- The reporter tactfully summarizes the students' goals from their perspective. They wish to form a "stu-

dent union." And their purpose in demanding to wear dashikies, he says, is to acquire more "black influence" in the school. This suggests "cultural influence," since dashikies are a native African fashion. But dashikies are also a black-power symbol, and the "influence" sought here is the influence of an all-black "union." The reporter's sympathetic euphemism blurs the actual goals of the militants, and constitutes a covert advocacy of black racism. The reporter would not so tactfully blur the goals of a white racist group that sought to wear garb symbolizing white racism and to form a "union" to expand their "influence."

• The reporter's description of the violence that breaks out is a veritable orgy of passive verbs—an abnormal usage that leaves in total obscurity the answers to such questions as: Who provoked the violence? And: Who was victimized by the violence? As written, a "protest" suddenly "spilled over" into the streets—Embodied... by whom? Initiated... by whom? Stones "were thrown"... by whom? Bottles "were thrown"... by whom? Windows "were broken"... by whom? There was similar "trouble" elsewhere—"trouble" involving... whom? Initiated... by whom? Some twenty persons were injured... by whom?

There are only two sentences in this entire section in which subjects and objects are crystal clear: "Several hundred protesters were confronted by police in blue uniforms and police recruits in khaki." And: "The demonstrators, in turn, charged police brutality."

In fact, in this entire description of a violent riot, only one sentence uses an active verb. Namely: The black militants *"charged"* the police with brutality. It appears that only where police culpability is alleged does the CBS reporter regain control of direct English usage.

The effect of this syntactical double standard is to blur the guilt of the black rioters for an outbreak of violence, and to place the police "confrontation" and the charge of "police brutality" in abnormally sharp focus.

- The riot is misreported in yet another way: It is an irresponsible euphemism to describe as "unrest" a riot in which property was destroyed, many people injured and life was lost. It results in the glamorization of the black-power rioters and "restless" kids.
- After allowing a critic of the black-power militants to speak, the reporter instantly resumes the rioters' perspective, in his own narrative. He reports on the emotions of "many" of the black students which he has, presumably, plumbed by mind-reading: "There was some sense of wonder at it all." What does the reporter mean by this? One has to read the following quote from a black student to discover: The student says hippies come to school in beads, so why can't blacks wear dashikies? The reporter does not say if the school authorities, the victims of the riot or the family of the dead person also find the situation "wondrous."
- Finally, the reporter concludes this story, describing this riot as a culmination of the "agony" of the civil rights movement. He thus casts the history of Negro suffering like a historical cloak over this particular outbreak. And, in his last word, he repeats the rioters' self-justifications for their violence as fact: "What is at stake is a matter of black identity, black pride, and how the Negro students choose to express it." This is the ultimate justification and glamorization of the black-power rioters and of their violence.

Story Number Three (Excluded from the CBS Study)

This story is still more covert in its approach to violence. No reference to it appears in the story at all—by the reporter's choice.

TNT SUMMARY

10/31: The reporter purports to summarize Cleaver's political position, and glamorizes him as a simple integrationist—by omitting any reference to Cleaver's advocacy of murder of whites, police, businessmen, etc. (*TNT*, page 71).

CBS BROADCAST

(*The reportorial narrative which contains the opinion is italicized.*) This is the first half of a long story, in which CBS reports on several presidential candidates of minority parties:

> Reporter: As everybody knows it's a three-man presidential race this year. Three candidates are on every ballot. Three candidates show strength in the polls, three candidates are in the news every night. But if it's really a three-man race, what about Eldridge Cleaver?
>
> Cleaver: (...) You have a choice between Oink, Oink and Oink.
>
> Reporter: *Eldridge Cleaver is on the ballot in five states as candidate of the Peace and Freedom Party (...) against the Vietnam war. Cleaver is an ex-convict, information minister of the Black Panther movement and author of the best-selling book,* Soul on Ice. *He preaches contempt for the white power structure, but unlike some black militants, he believes in working with sympathetic whites.*
>
> Cleaver: (...) has the opportunity to form a coalition with white people in the Peace and Freedom Party who recently (...) our racial tensions and have created a framework in which black people and white people will try to deal with the situation and work together. We think that this is a very positive development and we are seeking to exploit it from California to the rest of the country, and we know that they need us.
>
> Reporter: We mentioned that Cleaver is the candidate of the Peace and Freedom party and he is in some states, but in some other states comedian Dick Gregory represents the Peace and Freedom party, except in New York where he represents the Freedom and Peace party, a splinter group. At times Gregory's speeches reflect (...) as a nightclub comedian. He notes the relative lack of rioting this year.

Gregory: (...) the army this year, that they didn't call out during the expected season, July through August. We were at home reading our consumer reports. We ain't going to steal bad stuff no more.

Reporter: But Gregory can be serious too. *And where Eldridge Cleaver denounces the police as pigs, Gregory calls for higher pay for policemen.*

TEXTUAL ANALYSIS

The essence of the slanting in this story emerges from omission of material that is rationally relevant to the theme of the story—the political views of a presidential candidate. The reporter presumes to summarize the essence of Eldridge Cleaver's political position. He includes the information that Cleaver is an ex-convict, "information minister" of the Black Panther movement, an "author" and an opponent of the Vietnam war. He excludes the information that Cleaver is a Marxist, dedicated by his own say-so, to the destruction of U.S. capitalism, and that he is a constant advocate of political violence.

The reporter's elaboration of Cleaver's political views is evasive and euphemistic. His first point is that Cleaver, although he "preaches contempt" for the "white power structure," "believes in working with sympathetic whites." This suggests a nonviolent attitude on Cleaver's part, and a desire to work within the system for the solution of racial problems.

The reporter then suggests that the principal object of Cleaver's "contempt" is the police.

Both of these points can only be made by virtue of the active suppression of Cleaver's actual views.

The producer of CBS's News show, if not this reporter, was certainly aware of what Cleaver's real views were. On 9/18, CBS put a segment of a political speech by Cleaver on the air—in which the nature of Cleaver's "contempt" for the "white power structure" is made clear. In this speech, Cleaver calls for the *murder* of big businessmen, politicians and agents of the police. They must be disposed of, says Cleaver; they must be "shot." The 9/18 story says that Cleaver has made these statements "again and again."[7]

To portray a continual advocate of political murder—by CBS's own say-so—as "author," as "information minister," as an opponent of the Vietnam war, and as a simple integrationist who is bitter about the cops; to summarize his calls for political murder as "contempt" for the "white power structure"; and to cite a few "Oinks" and an innocuous passage on racial cooperation from Cleaver, as evidence of what he stands for—is distortion by omission, a journalistic vice equivalent to "lying by omission."

It is to glamorize an advocate of political violence.

Story Number Four (Cited in the CBS Study)

This is the story where Cleaver issues his call for political murder. The reporter's narrative here is the most guarded, covert, and subtle of all.

TNT SUMMARY

    9/18: The reporter covertly glamorizes Eldridge Cleaver after Cleaver demands that big businessmen, politicians, police and profitmakers be disposed of and "shot." The reporter uses euphemistic descriptions of Cleaver's advocacy of murder, calling it "tough talk"; attacks those who refuse to hire Cleaver as "censors"; and reports no criticism of Cleaver's calls for political murder (*TNT*, page 71).

CBS BROADCAST

(The reportorial narrative which contains the opinion is italicized.)

> **Reporter:** *The student protests of five years ago brought many changes to the university (Berkeley), including more voice for students and faculty in setting up new classes. Now sharp controversy over a course on the American social order, with the guest lecturer anti-establishment black revolutionary Eldridge Cleaver.*
>
> **Cleaver:** It's the big businessmen, the politicians and these career military and police agent type people that,

this power structure we talk about, the people who have a vested interest in the status quo, who draw their living from exploiting people through this economic system, people who live by this profit, not the people who are just plugged into the system and who have a job and go to work every day and really never manage to get their head above water. But it's the power people, the people who make the decisions in this country and who control the decision-making process in this country. Those are the enemies of the people, and those are ones who are going to be exposed and treated in a manner that they're always treated in a revolutionary situation.

Reporter: "They ought to be shot." Cleaver has said that again and again. When whites ask what they can do for race relations, Cleaver has said, "Give black men machine guns." *For ten lectures Cleaver is to get no state salary, but will be paid from student funds. His tough talk prompted the state senate to censure the university, and brought criticism from two men who otherwise rarely agree.*

Governor Ronald Reagan: I'm opposed from the simple standpoint that I think it is ridiculous to bring someone on as a supposed instructor or lecturer, which is the way he was to be brought on, who has absolutely no qualifications whatsoever for that position.

Jesse Unruh: I think clearly it's very, very difficult to defend the appointment of Mr. Cleaver as a lecturer. I think that it's an unfortunate choice and represents almost a death wish on the part of those people participating in it insofar as the university is concerned.

Reporter: *Cleaver is thirty-three. He's done time on narcotics and assault convictions and was in court this week on fresh charges of assault and attempted murder. He faces trial for that later in the year. But the university regents meet tomorrow to consider demands they overrule the selection of Cleaver as guest lecturer.*

TEXTUAL ANALYSIS

There is scarcely an idea in the reporter's narrative which is not implicitly favorable to Cleaver—in contrast to alternative views which exist on the subject. Virtually every one of the few reportorial sentences requires analysis.

- The core quote around which this story is built is Cleaver's overt call for the extermination of every one in this country with power—political and economic. Cleaver—to use non-euphemistic language—is calling for political mass murder.
- The reporter sets this core quote in a context of intellectual freedom and progress. He says that student protests of five years ago have brought "more voice for students and faculty in setting up new classes." This suggests that the presence of Cleaver, who is giving one of these "new classes," is a manifestation of the new intellectual freedom.

  This is a debatable opening statement, since there are many, including Berkeley academicians, who see the earlier "student protests"—i.e., the "Dirty Speech Movement"—as having inaugurated a steady deterioration of the university, and who see Cleaver's presence as an expression of that deterioration.
- In his very next sentence, the reporter tacitly adopts the pro-Cleaver perspective—by describing him, without qualification, as a "guest lecturer" who is giving a course on "the American social order." Opponents of Cleaver do not view him as an intellectual, or as a man qualified to lecture on "the American social order" at an American university.
- In the same sentence, the reporter also adopts the pro-Cleaver perspective on his political role: He describes Cleaver as a "revolutionary." This, too, is a controversial description. Many would deny the existence of a revolutionary situation in the U.S. since the majority of U.S. citizens are profoundly recalcitrant to the concept of the violent overthrow of the American government or "system." Those who deny a revolu-

tionary situation do not describe Cleaver as a revolutionary.

• Having cast Cleaver as a "revolutionary intellectual," the reporter then proceeds to let Cleaver express some of his "revolutionary thought," which, the reporter says, Cleaver expresses constantly: Cleaver calls for disposing of "decision-makers, profit-makers," etc., "shooting" them, and demands "machine guns."

• Right after Cleaver's call for mass murder, the reporter makes yet another controversial decision: He could clarify the moral meaning of Cleaver's words—by the simple means of stating that this *is* a call for mass murder. Instead, he chooses to dim the meaning by switching rapidly to trivia: He chats about Cleaver's salary as a "lecturer."

• The reporter then refers to the Cleaver statements as "tough talk." This is a remarkable euphemism for a call for mass murder. Indeed, "tough talk," when applied to a political figure, is normally a form of praise. It means he is a man who names the issues courageously. This is tacit glamorization of Cleaver.

• The reporter next cites two mild criticisms of Cleaver. He either does not seek to elicit strong opinions—or he chops them out of the film in the cutting room. The critics' opinions are not directed to the central element of the Cleaver controversy—namely: Is a man who habitually advocates murder as social policy qualified to lecture on the American "social order"? Had the reporter wanted direct views on this subject, he could have gotten them by the bushel.

• At the very end of this story—tacked on as a postscript—the reporter mentions that Cleaver has "done time on narcotics and assault charges"—a gentle way to describe a self-proclaimed rapist—and that he "was in court this week on fresh charges of assault and attempted murder." Had these facts been presented at the outset, they would have had a deglamorizing effect on the rest of the story. The calls for murder by a man about to be tried for attempted murder would sound substantially less "revolutionary" and more criminal. By giving this information as a disintegrated postscript, the reporter is supporting his covert view of Cleaver as a "revolutionary thinker" and not as a criminal.

* Finally, the reporter—and I must repeat the sentence—says this: "... (Cleaver) was in court this week on fresh charges of assault and murder. He faces trial for that later in the year. *But* the university regents meet tomorrow to consider demands they overrule the selection of Cleaver as a guest lecturer" (emphasis added).

The clear-cut implication of the "But" is that the university regents are jumping the gun—that they should wait until Cleaver is found guilty or not guilty. With this last suggestion that the regents are unjust, the reporter once again reveals his pro-Cleaver sympathies, and terminates his story.

Summary: In the context of this story built around a call for mass murder, this consistent choice of the muted formulations must be described as covert but systematic sanctioning of Cleaver—and a glamorization of his violent appeals for mass murder as "revolutionary thought."

How the CBS Study Deals with Black Militants

Of the four possible stories to select for the CBS study, CBS chooses the last, number four. CBS then omits critical information pertaining to *TNT*'s analysis of this story:

* CBS does not isolate or italicize the relevant sections of the story—although it claims in its introduction to the CBS study that it has identified the "pertinent portions" of the broadcast. The reader of the CBS study cannot know that *TNT* is only classifying *eight* sentences of reportorial narrative.
* In reporting on *TNT*'s analysis of the story, CBS cites the one-sentence appendix statement as if it were a summary of *overt* content, italicizing it misleadingly, as follows:

> *Appendix I: Reporter sanctions Cleaver's calls for mass murder* as "revolutionary" thought and attacks those who would prevent Cleaver from teaching at Berkeley as "censors."

CBS presents this as a glaring absurdity. CBS fails to inform the reader of the CBS study that this is a summary of *implications*—of *covert* meanings.

> • CBS withholds the more detailed *TNT* summary on page 71 which makes quite clear that *TNT* is discussing a *covert* phenomenon—that implications, euphemisms, and evasions are issues in *TNT*'s analysis—to repeat:

TNT: The reporter *covertly glamorizes* Eldridge Cleaver after Cleaver demands that big businessmen, politicians, police and profitmakers be disposed of and "shot." The reporter uses *euphemistic descriptions* of Cleaver's advocacy of murder, calling it "tough talk"; attacks those who refuse to hire Cleaver as "censors"; and *reports no criticism of Cleaver's calls for political murder.* [Emphasis added.]

> • Finally, CBS tries to magnify the significance of a word error in this story. A typist did mistake "censures" for "censors," and the concept was used in the summaries, but the error is insignificant: it does not alter the pro-black militant classification, the word count, or the analysis of tacit glamorization of a violence-advocate. The error will be removed in the next edition, and nothing of significance will have altered.

The most revealing thing about CBS' approach to this story, however, is that CBS chooses it at all.

This choice is a necessity, if CBS is to challenge one story in the black militant category—the alternatives are too crude: the portrait of an innocuous Cleaver, asking only for cooperation with sympathetic whites . . . the black riot story, featuring dashikies, destruction and death, climaxed with ritual gushing about black pride . . . and the report which compulsively chants hero-hero-hero while a black-power advocate threatens to set cities aflame ... none of these are satisfactory for CBS's purposes.

CBS's purpose is to claim that "there is no justification whatever" to *TNT*'s charges that CBS newsmen sanctioned political violence. For that, the subtlest of the four stories is an absolute—an absolute sheltered by a series of misrepresentations.

Wallace

In *TNT*, the following statement appears (page 58):

> Network men covertly encouraged physical violence directed at Wallace.
>
> They did so by a specific set of euphemisms. Language customarily used to describe those who engage in verbal protest was used to describe those who engaged in physical assault. This was a tacit sanctioning of the assaultive conduct.
>
> This linguistic device in use on all three networks is highly significant coming as it does from men with large and varied vocabularies and men who are well able to distinguish between a verbal criticism and an act of physical violence. Certainly, network men have never in a burst of collective imprecision referred to club-swinging policemen—or, more recently, fist-swinging construction workers—as men engaging in verbal expression or men simply manifesting their intellectual disagreements. And yet network reporters insistently described people as intellectual or verbal dissenters at the precise moment when these people were engaging in physical acts of violence—thus systematically blurring the existential, moral and legal distinction between physical attack and verbal dissent.
>
> Over and over again, by this false equation of speech and force, these reporters were subtly, but repeatedly broadcasting the message that bodily assault and violence were just another form of "dissent" and that

throwing cans and rocks was an accredited and constitutionally protected verbal form of expression ... if the target was George Wallace.

Here, so that the pattern can be clearly recognized, are the *TNT* summaries (pages 58-60) of the stories on all three networks.

ABC

10/22/5 (Anti-Wallace): Opponents of Wallace throw eggs, vegetables and fruit at Wallace. The reporter calls them "hecklers."

10/23/6 (Anti-Wallace): Opponents throw objects including eggs, vegetables, fruit and stones at Wallace. One stone strikes Wallace in the face. The reporter calls these opponents "hecklers" and says, amusingly, evoking an old folk rhyme, that they threw "sticks, stones and names" at Wallace. He thus equates physical violence and words.

10/31/6 (Anti-Wallace): A group disrupts a Wallace rally, throws rocks, and hits two girls on the head. The reporter calls the group "demonstrators."

CBS

9/30/4 (Anti-Wallace): The story states that an opponent of Wallace threw an egg at him. The reporter's description is: "The dissenters made their presence known."

10/22/6 (Anti-Wallace): Opponents throw rocks at George Wallace. The reporter calls them "hecklers."

10/23/4 (Anti-Wallace): Black-power opponents of George Wallace throw "objects" at him. The reporter describes this as Wallace's being "heckled."

NBC

10/17/8 (Anti-Wallace): Opponents of Wallace throw tin cans at him. The reporter refers to this as "disruption" of Wallace's speech—thus describing violence directed at a human being as if it were the interruption of a speech.

10/22/10 (Anti-Wallace): The reporter describes

George Wallace as being "heckled mercilessly" and as being hit with an "apple core" flung by the "hecklers."

10/23/3 (Anti-Wallace): The reporter says college students threw objects at Wallace. He sums it up as: "letting Wallace know what they think of him"—thus describing physical violence as if it were an expression of "thought."

10/31/8 (Anti-Wallace): Demonstrators hurl objects at Wallace. The reporter describes it as "they heckled and threw things." This is the only formulation that makes a distinction between speech and physical violence, but it is still a remarkably casual way of describing the phenomenon.

Here is the text of the three CBS stories in particular—with the relevant passages italicized.

Story Number One (Excluded from the CBS Study)

CBS BROADCAST
(9/30) This is the middle section of a long story on George Wallace—the sound track indistinct in places, due to the booing.

> **Reporter:** His motorcade today through Chicago's Loop was impressive. His crowds were neither as large nor as loud as those who turned out for Nixon, but the third party candidate's route was shorter both in distance and in size. Like most such events, it was time for the lunch hour on State Street. He traveled the eight-block distance in a matter of twenty minutes. (. . .) *The dissenters made their presence known. Some threw confetti; one threw an egg.*

Story Number Two (Cited in the CBS Study)

CBS BROADCAST
(10/22) This is a short story on George Wallace, including Wallace's reaction to the attacks on him.

At a rally in Oshkosh, Wisconsin today, hecklers threw rocks, eggs and tomatoes at George Wallace. When (. . .) struck him on the shoulder, Wallace dismissed it with a remark, "That's all right. It'll wash off. That's just a bunch of anarchists."

Story Number Three (Excluded from the CBS Study)

CBS BROADCAST
 (10/23) Here is the anchorman's introduction, plus a section taken from a long story on Wallace, which includes Wallace's reaction to the attacks on him.

Anchorman: *In Ohio today, George Wallace found himself heckled by black power demonstrators and again the target of (. . .) and other objects.* In addition the former Alabama governor faced some questions about comments made by his running mate. . . .

Wallace: I can't tell the jeers from the cheers in that crowd out there but (. . .) Pretty hard. Pretty difficult. All right, go ahead and throw something else. You're brave throwing things. Let's (. . .) throw something else.

Reporter: At one point a Wallace supporter tore a sign from a heckler's hand. Police tore him from the crowd.

TEXTUAL ANALYSIS
 None is needed. The entire issue is one of euphemisms—in this case, language appropriate to intellectual disagreements being used to veil acts of violence.
 In *The Careful Writer*, subtitled, *A Modern Guide to English Usage*, by Theodore Bernstein, assistant managing editor of the *New York Times*, a "euphemism" is defined as follows: "A euphemism is a word or phrase that affords a way of getting around saying something unpleasant. . . . Euphemisms are not fig leaves, intended to hide something; they are diaphanous veils, intended to soften grossness or starkness."

In the examples given, the CBS reporters, like the reporters on the other two networks, are doing precisely this: They are trying to evade the "unpleasantness," and "soften" the starkness" of "demonstrators' " physical violence directed against Wallace.

In other words: they are verbally protecting them from having the nature of their actions named precisely. "Violence" is the concept the reporters are seeking to evade—and to "soften." This is, definitionally, a sanctioning of such conduct: it benefits only the violent. In CBS, as in the other two networks, the euphemisms for violence are solely used to evade violence by the blacks and the left. Violence by others—i.e., "police brutality"—is named starkly.[8]

How the CBS Study Deals with Wallace

The political significance of *TNT*'s charge that reporters used euphemisms for acts of violence against Wallace is quite simple to explain provided (1) one presents *TNT*'s brief explanation completely, and (2) one offers a *group* of examples to show the pattern.

CBS, however, does not want to explain it to the reader of the CBS Study. CBS wipes out both *TNT*'s reasoning *and* pattern.

- CBS omits all but the third and fourth sentences in *TNT*'s description of this euphemistic pattern; leaves out the concept that it is covert; leaves out all reasoning; leaves out all reference to the one-sided political use of euphemisms for violence; and above all, leaves out the concept of "euphemisms" itself. To wit:

This is another example of a sweeping, highly accusatory but unfounded charge. Miss Efron states (page 61) that network coverage of the George Wallace campaign "editorially sanctions the physical attacks upon him." In support of this serious accusation, she states (page 58) that "language customarily used to describe those who engage in verbal protest was used to describe those who engage in physical assault." This, she concludes, was "a tacit sanctioning of the assaultive conduct."

- CBS fails to present a group of examples which would allow a reader of the CBS study to see the tri-network euphemistic pattern and judge its significance. Instead, CBS tacitly denies the existence of a pattern by presenting only *one* story.
- CBS chooses the story which is best calculated to minimize the seriousness of *TNT*'s charge—the one in which Wallace *laughs off* the fact that he was struck by an apple core. Significantly, CBS does not cite the story where he is under severe physical attack by black-power militants and taunts them as cowards—while the CBS anchorman describes him as being "heckled."
- Even in presenting the one Wallace story, CBS does not isolate or italicize the relevant euphemistic passage, although it boasts in the introduction that it has identified the "pertinent portion of each broadcast." It presents a complete Wallace story followed by a complete Curtis LeMay story about integration in the armed services—both full of material irrelevant to the issue, i.e., to the *unidentified* issue of euphemisms (see Appendix B).
- Having deprived the reader of the CBS study of any way to assess *TNT*'s charges, CBS then "argues" as follows:

> In any event, it is hardly realistic or accurate to conclude that use of the terms "hecklers" and "dissidents" constituted an *"editorial sanction"* of physical attacks upon Mr. Wallace—particularly since each of the broadcasts explicitly reported the physical acts involved.

This is equivocation. The covert sanctioning of violence by reporters is not disproved by arguing that they "report" on physical attacks. The issue is *how* they report on these attacks, how they identify such attacks, whether these identifications are euphemistic or not, and whether such euphemisms are used on both sides of the political fence.

That is the basic question raised by *TNT*—the question that CBS evades, camouflages and never answers.

Conclusion

The CBS study did one final thing to obliterate the picture of how CBS News dealt with the issue of political violence.

It cited Wallace story number 2 in full and black-militant story number 4 in full—isolating no sections of these stories whatever—and declared them to be "representative." "Representative" of what? CBS did not say.

This was CBS's ultimate attempt to wipe out the existent violence-sanctioning patterns as reported by *TNT* and as demonstrated in this chapter, and to substitute a non-pattern in their place.

Ultimately, a non-pattern is chaos. And the reader of this report is advised to examine the incoherence of the CBS study's section on violence. It is the inevitable consequence of CBS's irrational goal—disintegration of *TNT*'s violence charges, charges it could not refute after "inspecting" its own nine stores.

---

[1] Opinion on "Demonstrators" includes opinion on "activists," "militants," "students," "hippies," etc., provided these have no explicit political identification as leftists or radicals or black militants.

[2] In excerpts from network transcripts:
    (. . .) indicates unintelligibility on tape.
    . . . indicates material not on subject.
Because of the limitations of home-recording equipment, transcripts may contain occasional word errors. The context, however, provides a suitable test for the coherence of the ideas.

³All textual analyses in this book come from *TNT* research. The research was offered in *TNT* to all readers. CBS never requested the research, thus omitted all such analyses from its study of *TNT*'s analytical process.

⁴That CBS will go to cynical lengths to protect its claim to be innocent of such editorial practices was made luminously clear on October 11—the publication date of *TNT* and the release date of the CBS study—when the author of *TNT* was interviewed on CBS-owned WCAU in Philadelphia by CBS man Joel Spivak. Mr. Spivak announced on that program that *TNT* was in substantial accord with his own experience of network news bias. *TNT*'s author then read, over the air, the analysis of the above story. In response, CBS locked up the tape of this program and refused to release the transcript.

⁵It was also classified as "anti-middle class" (see page 69 of this report). Opinion on Agnew, as such, was not classified.

⁶This is one example of a group of four, where CBS misrepresented *TNT*'s qualitative statements in order to pit them against *TNT* statistics. For other examples, see pages 123, 127, and 129 of this report.

⁷See next story. The chronology of these stories has been reversed because they are being presented in order of progressive subtlety.

⁸For a striking example of a reporter's linguistic shift from verbal evasion of black violence to sharply focused language when it comes to police violence, see page 31 of this report.

II. Left

In the area of opinion on the left, CBS's "spot check" lands with apparent capriciousness on outright minutiae; the CBS study selects only three items:

1) *TNT*'s interpretation of Sevareid's use of the word "big."
2) One mistake in a word.
3) One overlooked opinion.

Given the nature and controversiality of the radical movement of 1968, and the number of *TNT* pages—forty (exclusive of appendices)—on coverage of the left and related issues, this selection of items is more than curious.

Here are the CBS challenges—as the CBS study presents them. Each is followed by an analysis.

Item Number One

The CBS study says:

10/7/68 The reporter, who is analyzing the Wallace campaign, states:

"In a real sense the Wallace movement represents a class struggle, an uprising against what he calls the pseudo-intellectuals, professors, preachers, and everything that is big—government, taxes, ownership, the big press, the big networks, the Negro movement, the left-wing student movement. All this is summed up in the word 'they'. 'It is them against us, and,' says Wallace, 'there are more of us than of them.'"

Appendix J (page 326): Miss Efron sees in this report a "pro-left editorial" by the reporter because he "describes left-wing student movement as one of the biggest institutions in the country."

This presentation is a tissue of petty misrepresentations:

- CBS says *TNT* describes this report as a "pro-left editorial." *TNT* does not say this; the issue is that of covert opinion from an *editorial source*. (See any *TNT* appendix.)
- CBS pretends to give "Miss Efron's" reason for this classification by citing the summarized opinion in Appendix J. The Appendix gives no reason; it merely states the opinion. The reason, however, *is* given clearly on page 111 where the covert character of the opinion is analyzed. CBS leaves this out:

The reporter describes the minority left-wing student movement as "big" and compares it to "big government," "big taxes," "the big press," and "the big networks" *thus inflating its significance.* [Emphasis added.]

"Inflation of significance" is a form of *glamorization*, identified in *TNT* (page 111) as a covert slanting technique. CBS flatly excludes all reference to it.

CBS is attempting to make *TNT*'s textual analysis seem arbitrary and unfounded.

TEXTUAL ANALYSIS

This is a report from Eric Sevareid which purports to tell us the "meaning" of the Wallace movement. He quotes Wallace to document his point that the Wallace movement is a struggle against everything that is "big," including the left-wing student movement.

In fact, Wallace says the opposite. Wallace is not describing the left-wing student movement or any other of the listed phenomena as "big." He is saying they are less "big" than the Wallace movement—that "there are more of us than of them."

Sevareid is using Wallace as a cover to express his own opinion about the "bigness" of all the objects of Wallace's attack. He is therefore directly responsible for the description of the left-wing student movement as one of the biggest institutions in the United States—comparable in scope and significance to the "government."

This is inflated description of the importance of student radicals in 1968.

TNT cites Kenneth Crawford in *Newsweek* magazine (June 2, 1968) on an Elmo Roper study of political attitudes on U.S. campuses. He reports that the poll "shows that the noisy militants one reads so much in the newspapers and sees so much of on television constitute a less-than-10-percent minority." The Gallup and Harris polls of a year later also confirm the fact that the radical movement was a less-than-10-percent campus movement.

This is why *TNT* describes the Sevareid statement as a false magnification of this movement—and consequently an expression of glamorizing pro-left opinion.

Item Number Two

The CBS study says:
  Miss Efron makes charges based on alleged but nonexistent statements in the CBS News broadcasts.

Miss Efron writes (page 90):
  "CBS initially relates the tale of how Muskie invited one of a group of 'leftists' to the platform. (9/25/7, Anti-Humphrey.) About nine days later CBS forgets that they were leftists. The reporter recalls that when 'stop-the-war' students heckled Muskie, he was willing to listen—but that Muskie is far less courteous to Wallace hecklers. And the CBS reporter asks Muskie why he

is more impatient with 'Wallace hecklers' than with 'young, restless hecklers.' Thus the 'leftists' change into 'stop-the-war' students and then into a touching group known as 'young, restless hecklers.' (CBS, 10/4/12, Pro-'Demonstrators.')"

Miss Efron's conclusion that the 10/4/12 report constituted a pro-demonstrators editorial is based on an alleged reference, in the October 4, 1968 broadcast, to "young, *restless* hecklers." (Emphasis added.) There was no such reference. The actual reference was "young, leftist hecklers."

Her misunderstanding of this word has led her mistakenly to charge (pages 89, 92) that CBS News editorialized by "suppressing" the political or ideological identity of hecklers and demonstrators. (Emphasis added.)

Assuming the error as stated by CBS, this criticism is preposterous.

TNT has charged the three networks with systematically suppressing the leftist identity of 1968 hecklers and demonstrators. CBS is saying that *TNT*'s case rests on a *single word* in a single CBS story—and that an error in that word wipes out the entire case.

CBS carefully omits all reference to the pattern of suppression identified in *The News Twisters*, and avoids citation of all the pages that contain the evidence. The evidence is first presented and interpreted in detail on pages 76, 77, 78, 84, 85, 86, 87, 88, 89, 90, 91, 92, 93. The book also refers the reader to Appendix K for a complete line-up of stories on all three networks in which the political identity of "demonstrators" is omitted. Here is Appendix K in full:

STORY NO.	SOURCE OF OPINION	Pro-Demonstrators† ABC
9/24/11	Editorial	Reporter supports demonstrators (demonstrators politically unidentified).
	Public	Student supports demonstrators (demonstrators politically unidentified).

LEFT 53

9/25/9	Public	Student heckler attacks U.S. political system (demonstrators politically unidentified).
9/26/5	Editorial	Reporter supports demonstrators (demonstrators politically unidentified).*
9/30/2	Editorial	Reporter supports demonstrators (demonstrators politically unidentified).*
10/7/5	Editorial	Reporter supports demonstrators (demonstrators politically unidentified).
10/8/10	Editorial	Reporter supports demonstrators (demonstrators politically unidentified).*
10/9/6	Candidate	Humphrey supports demonstrators (demonstrators politically unidentified).
10/24/8	Editorial	Reporter supports demonstrators (demonstrators politically unidentified).*
10/24/9	Public	Student protest leader supports demonstrators (demonstrators politically unidentified).*
	Editorial	Reporter supports demonstrators (demonstrators politically unidentified).
10/29/5	Editorial	Reporter supports demonstrators (demonstrators politically unidentified).
10/30/9	Editorial	Reporter supports demonstrators (demonstrators politically unidentified).

STORY NO.	SOURCE OF OPINION	CBS
9/30/2	Candidate	Humphrey supports demonstrators (demonstrators politically unidentified).
	Editorial	Reporter supports demonstrators (demonstrators politically unidentified).*
10/4/12	Candidate	Muskie supports demonstrators (demonstrators politically unidentified).
	Editorial	Reporter supports demonstrators (demonstrators politically unidentified).
10/14/8	Editorial	Reporter supports demonstrators (demonstrators politically unidentified).
	Editorial	Reporter supports demonstrators (demonstrators politically unidentified).*

10/15/3	Editorial		Reporter supports demonstrators (demonstrators politically unidentified).
10/23/9	Public		Leader of student demonstrations at Berkeley attacks establishment violence (demonstrators politically unidentified).

STORY NO.	SOURCE OF OPINION	NBC
9/23/12	Public	Activist student attacks U.S. political system (self-described radical, socialist, supporter of Eldridge Cleaver's Peace and Freedom Party).
	Editorial	Reporter supports demonstrators (demonstrators politically unidentified).
9/25/2	Public	Hecklers attack U.S. political system (demonstrators politically unidentified).
10/3/12	Editorial	Reporter supports demonstrators (demonstrators politically unidentified).*
10/8/11	Public	Student attacks U.S. political system (demonstrators politically unidentified).
	Public	Student attacks U.S. political system (demonstrators politically unidentified).
10/14/4	Editorial	Reporter supports demonstrators (demonstrators politically unidentified).*
10/16/9	Editorial	Reporter supports demonstrators (demonstrators politically unidentified).*
10/23/8	Public	Tom Hayden, of the SDS, attacks establishment violence (demonstrators politically unidentified).
10/23/14	Public	Artists attack establishment violence; condemn brutal repression of demonstrators (demonstrators politically unidentified).
10/30/10	Political	Ribicoff attacks establishment violence against "demonstrators" (demonstrators politically unidentified).
	Political	Ribicoff attacks establishment violence against "demonstrators" (demonstrators politically unidentified).

LEFT 55

Political	Ribicoff attacks establishment violence against "demonstrators" (demonstrators politically unidentified).
Public	Man congratulates Ribicoff for his defense of "demonstrators" (demonstrators politically unidentified).
Political	Ribicoff attacks Chicago police for brutality against "demonstrators" (demonstrators politically unidentified).

Anti-Demonstrators

STORY NO.	SOURCE OF OPINION	ABC
9/16/6	Candidate	Agnew attacks demonstrators for violence (demonstrators politically unidentified).
9/18/2B	Political	J. Edgar Hoover attacks demonstrators for violence (demonstrators politically unidentified).
9/19/1	Candidate	Humphrey attacks demonstrators (demonstrators politically unidentified).
9/20/8	Editorial	Reporter attacks demonstrators for violence (demonstrators politically unidentified).
9/24/11	Public	Students attack demonstrators (demonstrators politically unidentified).
	Public	Student attacks demonstrators (demonstrators politically unidentified).
9/25/9	Public	Rally speakers attack demonstrators (demonstrators politically unidentified).
9/26/5	Editorial	Reporter attacks demonstrators (demonstrators politically unidentified).
9/30/2	Candidate	Humphrey attacks demonstrators for violence (demonstrators politically unidentified).
10/2/4	Candidate	Wallace attacks demonstrators (demonstrators politically unidentified).
10/2/7	Candidate	Nixon attacks demonstrators for violence (demonstrators politically unidentified).

10/8/10	Editorial	Reporter attacks demonstrators (demonstrators politically unidentified).
10/15/4	Candidate	Wallace attacks demonstrators for violence (demonstrators politically unidentified).
10/15/5	Candidate	Agnew attacks demonstrators for violence (demonstrators politically unidentified).
10/17/8	Candidate	Wallace attacks demonstrators (demonstrators politically unidentified).
10/22/5	Candidate	Wallace attacks demonstrators (demonstrators politically unidentified).
10/24/9	Public	Policeman attacks demonstrators for violence (demonstrators politically unidentified).
10/24/12	Editorial	Reporter attacks demonstrators (demonstrators politically unidentified).
10/25/9	Candidate	Wallace attacks demonstrators (demonstrators politically unidentified).
10/30/9	Candidate	Agnew attacks demonstrators (demonstrators politically unidentified).
10/31/8	Public	Union man attacks demonstrators for violence (demonstrators politically unidentified).

STORY NO.	SOURCE OF OPINION	CBS
9/16/1	Candidate	Humphrey attacks demonstrators for violence (demonstrators politically unidentified).
9/17/4	Candidate	Humphrey attacks demonstrators (demonstrators politically unidentified).
9/18/2	Political	J. Edgar Hoover attacks demonstrators for violence (demonstrators politically unidentified).
9/19/1	Political	Senator Edward Kennedy attacks demonstrators for violence (demonstrators politically unidentified).
	Candidate	Humphrey attacks demonstrators (demonstrators politically unidentified).

LEFT 57

9/19/3	Candidate	Nixon attacks demonstrators (demonstrators politically unidentified).
9/20/10	Candidate	Wallace attacks demonstrators (demonstrators politically unidentified).
	Public	Workingmen attack demonstrators (demonstrators politically unidentified).
	Public	Union men attack demonstrators (demonstrators politically unidentified).
	Public	Union man attacks demonstrators (demonstrators politically unidentified).
9/24/9	Candidate	Humphrey attacks demonstrators for violence (demonstrators politically unidentified).
10/14/8	Candidate	Agnew attacks demonstrators for violence (demonstrators politically unidentified).
	Public	Middle-class whites attack demonstrators for violence (demonstrators politically unidentified).
10/16/11	Public	Chicago organization attacks demonstrators for violence (demonstrators politically unidentified).
10/21/11	Candidate	Wallace attacks demonstrators for violence (demonstrators politically unidentified).
10/22/13	Editorial	Reporter attacks demonstrators for violence (demonstrators politically unidentified).
10/23/9	Public	Hoffer attacks demonstrators (demonstrators politically unidentified).
10/30/7	Candidate	Nixon attacks demonstrators for violence (demonstrators politically unidentified).

		NBC
STORY NO.	SOURCE OF OPINION	
9/18/1	Political o	J. Edgar Hoover attacks demonstrators for violence (demonstrators politically unidentified).
9/19/1	Political	Senator Edward Kennedy attacks demonstrators for violence (demonstrators politically unidentified).

9/19/20	Political	Georgia officials attack demonstrators for violence (demonstrators politically unidentified).
9/20/2	Candidate	Humphrey attacks demonstrators (demonstrators politically unidentified).
9/20/3	Political	Lawrence O'Brien attacks demonstrators (demonstrators politically unidentified).
9/30/3	Candidate	Humphrey attacks demonstrators (demonstrators politically unidentified).
10/3/17	Political	Undercover agent attacks demonstrators for violence (demonstrators politically unidentified).
10/8/11	Political	Senator Kennedy attacks demonstrators (demonstrators politically unidentified).
10/10/13	Political	Ex-governor of South Dakota attacks demonstrators for violence (demonstrators politically unidentified).
10/14/4	Candidate	Agnew attacks demonstrators for violence (demonstrators politically unidentified).
10/15/10	Candidate	Agnew attacks demonstrators for violence (demonstrators politically unidentified).
10/18/6	Candidate	Wallace attacks demonstrators (demonstrators politically unidentified).
10/23/5	Candidate	Agnew attacks demonstrators (demonstrators politically unidentified).
10/23/8	Public	Hoffer attacks demonstrators (demonstrators politically unidentified).
10/24/11	Public	"Berkeley University" member attacks demonstrators for violence (demonstrators politically unidentified).
	Editorial	Reporter attacks demonstrators (demonstrators politically unidentified).
10/25/7	Candidate	Wallace attacks demonstrators (demonstrators politically unidentified).
10/30/8	Candidate	Agnew attacks demonstrators (demonstrators politically unidentified).
10/30/10	Political	Ed May, Connecticut state senator, attacks demonstrators (demonstrators politically unidentified).

10/31/8   Candidate   Wallace attacks demonstrators (demonstrators politically unidentified).

†In this section, opinions are summarized only as they deal with attacks on the U.S. political system and the "Establishment"; with violence; and with the identity of the "demonstrators."

*Editorial rationalization of violence; for summaries, see Chapter III section on "Demonstrators."

On the basis of this pattern of omission, *The News Twisters* makes the following charge: "During the seven weeks of coverage, opinion on 'demonstrators' appears ninety-five times and none of these 'demonstrators' has any specific political identity. Above all, none are described as 'leftists' " (page 78). If CBS is correct about the misunderstanding of one word in one story, this figure would have to be changed to ninety-four. And *TNT*'s charge that the three networks had systematically suppressed the role of the New Left in the political disturbances of 1968 would remain unaltered.

Since the CBS study was distributed from coast to coast, before *TNT*'s publication date, to people who had never laid eyes on *The News Twisters*, this attempt to hide nineteen pages of charges behind an error in one word is a solid example of "The Big Lie."

Item Number Three

TNT reports that during the period of study only two important opinions critical of violent radicals were aired—both from conservative sources—and only ABC covered both:

- 10/1: J. Edgar Hoover declared that the New Left in general and the Students for Democratic Society in particular were the main forces behind the outbreak of political violence in America. He reported that the New Left was planning sabotage and destruction for the future (*TNT*, pages 75, 76, 84).
- 10/3: A HUAC undercover investigator charged the Yippies with plans to bomb buildings, kill policemen and assassinate candidates (*TNT*, page 76).

Hoover

TNT states (page 76) that both CBS and NBC suppressed Hoover's report on present and future New Left and SDS violence. CBS does not comment on this.

HUAC

TNT states (page 76) that NBC covered the HUAC story but censored two of the three HUAC charges: the Yippie's alleged plans to kill policemen and to bomb buildings, reporting only on the alleged threat to kill all the presidential candidates.

But, according to *TNT*, CBS did not carry any of these charges. CBS challenges this fact, and claims, correctly, that it did. On October 3, 1968, CBS reported that "A witness told a congressional hearing today that Yippie leader Jerry Rubin talked of killing presidential candidates and overthrowing the government during the disorders accompanying the Democratic convention." This is an error, and *TNT* will rectify it in the next edition.

The rectification, however, will not do CBS much good: CBS suppressed the same two HUAC charges of plans for bombing and police-killing as those suppressed by NBC.

Conclusion

CBS is actually seeking to refute major, serious charges in *TNT*—without ever naming them. They are contained in a section of *TNT* (pages 84-93) called "Where are the Violent Radicals?" Here is the principal part of that entire section:

> *Where Are the Violent Radicals?*
>
> According to CBS, on October 7, 1968, the political grouping known as "the left-wing student movement" was one of the "big" American institutions—comparable, said the reporter, to "big government," "big taxes," "the big press," and "the big networks."
>
> The New Left indeed was so "big" according to the CBS reporter that it had intimidated much of the

American middle class and accounted in part for the sweep to George Wallace (CBS, 10/7/1, Pro-Left). These Americans, said CBS, didn't like "bigness."

About six days earlier, J. Edgar Hoover of the FBI had also declared the New Left to be "big." But he meant it in a quite different sense. The New Left, he said, was one of America's biggest problems. He declared that the New Left in general and the Students for a Democratic Society in particular were the main forces behind the tremendous outbreak of political violence in America. He reported that the New Left was planning sabotage and destruction for the future. In addition, the FBI charged that "foreign influences" were playing a significant role in the black leftist movement. (ABC, 10/1/11, Anti-Left.)

It wasn't the New Left's numerical "bigness" that was disturbing the Federal Bureau of Investigation in 1968. It was its lawlessness and violence. And, CBS to the contrary, it wasn't the New Left's numerical "bigness" that was disturbing the far "bigger" electorate and generating a "law and order" issue in the 1968 campaign: it was its lawlessness and violence. It was in 1968, as the current Scranton Report on Student Violence reminds us, that terrorist practices began: "Columbia 1968 injected elements of terror and property destruction." (*Newsweek*, October 5, 1970.)

Given the reported "bigness" of this political movement and its serious lawlessness, one would suppose that the networks would give the radicals "big" coverage. And one would suppose that a great deal of pro and con opinion would be found on the New Left as well as on its violence, and on the violence it was publicly pledging for the future.

Such is not the case.

There is, as we have seen, an extraordinary paucity of pro and con opinion on the left. What there is portrays the left as an innocuous group—a little bothersome, noisy, given to the use of odd words like "socialism," "imperialism," and "oink" but harmless nonetheless. On network TV, the left—save for two jarring intrusions by

J. Edgar Hoover and the HUAC—is shown as totally nonviolent.

And, as we have also seen, there is a great and mysterious reservoir of politically unidentified "youth," "students," "dissenters," "demonstrators," "activists" and "militants" who are not harmless at all and whose activities often take the form of the systematic violation of the rights of others, of assault and destruction, of rioting and burning and terrorism.

Who are these politically anonymous violent figures?

And where is the violent New Left?

The second question is answered more simply than the first. Although a large fraction of the country is intensely concerned with the issue of the violent radicals in 1968, and the subject is constantly aired in the press, almost nobody talks about it on network television—because network television does not *choose* to present the violent New Left as an issue of controversy.... And it is not opinion on violent radicals alone which was suppressed. It is the radicals themselves who have been obliterated. To an astonishing degree, this "big" American movement was kept under wraps by the networks.

We are left at the very end of this content analysis with: The Mystery of the Missing Radicals.

"Missing" is perhaps a misnomer. One cannot read network transcripts of this 1968 campaign period without an overpowering conviction that radicals in large numbers were being seen and heard on the news programs, incessantly assailing candidates and shouting against the war. And, indeed, this is the conviction of most Americans. Is this widespread belief reflected in the actual words said on the air?

No, it isn't.

The networks did cover the individuals and groups that militantly besieged and assaulted the candidates, and they described them for us. Who were they?

Here, taken from Appendix L, is a complete list of these sources of hostile public opinion as named by the reporters:

Opponents of Nixon and Agnew

ABC described them as: demonstrators; a student; hecklers; students

CBS described them as: grapeworkers; young Democrats; "someone"; students

NBC described them as: "someone"; hecklers; black militant; black militant; university students

Opponents of Humphrey and Muskie

ABC described them as: peace demonstrators; antiwar demonstrators; hecklers; antiwar demonstrators

CBS described them as: costumed demonstrators; young detractors and demonstrators; anti-Vietnam hecklers; "a few unfriendly signs in the crowd"; students

NBC described them as: dissenters and demonstrators; crowds; demonstrators; college students

Opponents of Wallace and LeMay

ABC described them as: protesters; hecklers; hecklers; hecklers; hecklers; hecklers; hecklers; hecklers; a protest group; college students and hecklers; demonstrators; jeerers and fighters

CBS described them as: dissenters; hecklers; hippie-heckler; hecklers; protesters; protesters; people of other persuasions; black people; Nixon supporters; black-power demonstrators and hecklers

NBC described them as: "stop-the-war demonstrators"; anti-Wallaceites; hecklers, mostly Negroes; hecklers; hecklers; protesters; young people; hecklers; hecklers; protesters in hippie garb and hecklers; "someone"; hecklers and demonstrators; hecklers, college students, militant Negroes

Opponents of All Three Candidates

ABC described them as: antiwar student; hecklers
CBS described them as: leaders of demonstrators who battled Chicago police during the Democratic convention; *a leftist*
NBC described them as: a stop-the-war demonstrator

In that total list, there is only one identified radical. CBS (9/25/7) describes *one* student who attacked all three candidates as a "leftist." According to NBC and ABC, those mobs denouncing and assaulting the Presidential candidates for seven weeks contained no radicals or New Leftists at all.

And what of the "antiwar" opinion? It, too, was covered by the networks and those who expressed such opinion were described. Who were they?

Here, taken from Appendix M, are all the sources of public opinion antagonistic to the war, as identified by the reporters:

Antiwar Groups

ABC described them as: peace demonstrators; antiwar student; antiwar demonstrators; antiwar demonstrators; pacifists; hecklers; hecklers; antiwar demonstrators; a would-be marcher; a soldier; actress Vanessa Redgrave; black militants
CBS described them as: leaders of Chicago demonstrators; demonstrators; anti-Vietnam hecklers; *a leftist student;* demonstrators; stop-the-war students; young restless hecklers; an organizer of the Chicago convention disorder
NBC described them as: a Connecticut matron; hecklers; a stop-the-war demonstrator; student; demonstrator; Jerry Rubin, a leader of Chicago antiwar demonstrators; an antiwar protest leader; a soldier; a leader of the 1966 student demonstrations at UCLA and

Berkeley; *Thomas Hayden of the Students for a Democratic Society;* President of Yale University; a group of artists

Here—in seven weeks of antiwar protest—we find *two* radicals. Or, to be precise, on CBS the *same* "left" student (9/25/7) who denounces the candidates also denounces the war; and on NBC (10/23/8) Tom Hayden of the SDS denounces the war. Actually, we have found only one new radical.

The almost total absence of individuals and groups editorially identified as New Leftists and radicals in precisely the areas where they operated most intensively in 1968 is a remarkable journalistic phenomenon indeed. It is particularly remarkable since network reporters show no diffidence in identifying Democrats, Republicans, Independent Party members, Black Panthers. McCarthyites, Kennedyites, socialists, UAW members, liberals, or conservatives.

One may conclude from The Mystery of the Missing Radicals that by a vast coincidence no network reporter ever happened to bump into a New Leftist although covering the candidates and antiwar demonstrators for seven weeks—or one may conclude that network reporters simply did not choose to identify New Leftists and radicals, in this context, and deliberately suppressed the information....

It seems fairly clear that the mysterious reservoir of politically anonymous violence is mysterious and anonymous only by virtue of such code language. There are no "missing radicals." What is missing is journalistic candor about the left.

In the last analysis, the three overlapping categories—the left, "demonstrators" and violent radicals—must be examined together, for they are an interlocked body of opinion. On three networks, reporters gave support to both the identified and unidentified left and its violence . . . sheltered it by euphemisms, and a set of graduated evasions ... systematically refused to condemn it ... and debated the major leaders of the country on its behalf. There is no doubt which side the networks sought to render more "forceful."

That is what CBS's "spot check" sought to answer with a quibble over the word "big," with a word error, and a missing opinion.

The items selected by the CBS "spot check" are mutely saying this:

1) Eric Severeid *didn't* say the left-wing student movement is "big"; Wallace did.

2) CBS *didn't* evade coverage of the left.

3) CBS *did* air criticism of the violent radicals.

To which the only reply is this:

1) Eric Sevareid did say the left-wing student movement is "big"; Wallace didn't.

2) Although CBS did identify two leftists in seven weeks—not one as *TNT* incorrectly reports—CBS did evade coverage of the left.

3) CBS did carry *one* story in which someone criticized the violent radicals on three counts—cutting out two of the three criticisms.

TNT's massive charges have been evaded. They have not been rebutted.

III. White Middle Class

Three times during the period of this study, CBS reporters tacitly linked the attribute of racism to the "white" middle class. This reportorial theme occurred on the other two networks as well—three times on NBC and twice on ABC, not to mention the two times that the charge was cited from non-reportorial sources on NBC.

A charge that was transmitted ten times in a seven-week period along with eleven other antagonistic estimates of the "white middle class" constitutes a pattern of some significance.

Again, CBS chooses to deny this—inevitably singling out for challenge the minutest and most subtle of the implicit editorial opinions carried on CBS. To illuminate CBS's selective processes, I present all three CBS illustrations of this implicit linkage of racism to the middle class.

Story Number One

Here is the subtle illustration CBS chooses to rebut. The CBS study says:

> 9/25/68 *CBS News Transcript:* "From Pennsylvania, Muskie flew to Michigan and there in Taylor, a white,

middle class suburb of Detroit, was heckled by supporters of George Wallace. Correspondent Herman reports that he handled them with as much aplomb as he handled college hecklers."

Appendix H (page 312) Miss Efron classifies this as an "anti-white middle-class editorial" by the reporter and comments: "Reporter attacks white middle class as racist."

Note that once again, CBS fails to identify the *TNT* statement as the summary of a *covert* attack; and fails to isolate the precise section, namely, the first sentence. The compliment to Muskie is irrelevant.

TEXTUAL ANALYSIS

The facts of the one-line "lead" simply indicate that some Wallace supporters heckled Muskie in a Detroit town named Taylor.

There was no logical reason for the reporter to bring up the whiteness or the middle-class status of the suburban neighborhood in which Muskie was heckled, since whiteness and middle-class status are the statistical norm in America, and are presumed unless explicitly denied. Similarly, whiteness and middle-class status are totally irrelevant to the Muskie heckling since white middle-class citizens voted for all presidential candidates.

Finally, Muskie, himself, is a member of the "white middle class," and would not be able to be elected without the support of the white middle-class majority.

The senselessness of this phrase is best grasped if one realizes that it would be most accurate to say: "White middle-class citizens who supported white middle-class Wallace heckled white middle-class Muskie in a white middle-class town." In the face of such a sentence, a white middle-class editor would cut out *all* references to "white middle class."

In this story, however, the reporter uses the reference in just one place. Since it is objectively meaningless, its only function is that of symbolism or code: The reporter inserted it as "background" for the only point of the story—Wallaceite hostility. Thus, the implication was smuggled in that the "white middle class" is Wallaceite—i.e., racist.

Story Number Two (Excluded from the CBS Study)

On 9/26, in a story describing a Nixon speech before a youth group, the CBS reporter says:

> Most of these youngsters are white middle class and Richard Nixon's strategy to win is based on the hope that their white middle-class parents are in the majority this year.

TEXTUAL ANALYSIS

As a purely factual description, this reference to the middle class is, again, senseless. White middle-class voters have always been in the majority in the United States; there is no need for Nixon to "hope" for this established demographic fact.

The reporter's statement is intelligible only by reference to the twice-repeated word "white," which suggests that Richard Nixon's real "hope" is to appeal to the "whiteness" of the majority, i.e., to its alleged racism.

Once again, this is code language—valuable for its covert meaning, since overtly it has none.

Story Number Three (Excluded from the CBS Study)

This story has already been reported on. It was cross-indexed as "pro-'demonstrators,' " and described as a carrier of tacit editorial support of political violence.

The only aspect of the editorializing which is relevant here is the covert charge that the white middle class is "racist."

On 10/14, a CBS reporter covers an Agnew campaign tour in the South "to win back votes, swayed by the segregationist rhetoric of George Wallace." The reporter recapitulates Agnew's reference to Poles as "Polacks" and his joke about a personal friend whom he called "the fat Jap." And the reporter states that throughout the campaign, "Agnew has hit many of the Wallace themes." These so-called Wallace themes include the need for termination of "violence," "student riots," urban disorder—"the need, in short, for law and order."

With this as context, the reporter states that Agnew's strength as a campaigner lies in the response he elicits from "ordinary middle-class whites" (the relevant section is italicized):

I like him, they murmur during the rally. I like what he says. They react because he is one of them, the kind of man who might be and was president of the local PTA. He shares their worries about what is happening to the white middle class, their fears of crime, of violent dissent and of militant class (...) He shares their limitations too, their short horizons. Agnew critics say that Agnew's strength as a campaigner is also his weakness as a vice-presidential candidate, as a man who could be president of the United States.

TEXTUAL ANALYSIS
- As the preceding context indicates, the introductory points of the reporter's narrative stress Agnew's "ethnic" blunders, and the espousal of what the reporter describes as "Wallace themes"—opposition to violence and lawlessness and the support of "law and order." To describe these as "Wallace" themes, when all presidential candidates took these positions, is to suggest covertly that Agnew's motive in espousing them is racist.
- The reporter then ties Agnew swiftly to his supporters, those who share his allegedly petty values—"ordinary middle-class *whites.*" In association with the prior racist charges against Agnew, this suggests that the "middle class" is responding in terms of its "whiteness," hence supports Agnew out of racism. Once again, the racist-class link is senseless. "Ordinary middle-class whites" include both racists and non-racists, and supported *all* candidates.
- Finally, after a variety of condescending comments, the reporter asserts that the "white middle class" has "limitations" and "short horizons." This implies that all Negroes, rich whites and acutely impoverished whites do not have "limitations"—another senseless notion.

All this is simply "racist" code talk of the most puerile kind, dressed up as dime-store sociology.

In summary: CBS reporters have linked the "middle class" to racism. Of the three possible illustrations of this pattern which CBS could challenge, it chooses the most subtle and avoids the more obvious.

It is not irrelevant to CBS' avoidance that the two more obvious examples also strongly intimate that Nixon and Agnew are racists.

IV. Conservatives

The CBS "spot check" lands on only one item in the area of opinion on conservatives. It is not a challenge of content. Here is what the CBS study says:

> *9/16/68 CBS News Transcript:* Humphrey: "The Rap Browns, the Stokely Carmichaels, the extremists of the left and the right will not have their way, and we will not allow them to terrorize or stampede America or cause us to lose our sense of perspective."
>
> *Appendix G (page 309)* Miss Efron classifies Mr. Humphrey's reference to extremists of the right as an "anti-conservative" attack. Her comment is: "Humphrey attacks *extremists* of the right for violence." (Emphasis added.) It is her judgment that an attack on "*extremists* of the right" is equivalent to an attack on "conservatives."

This is a severe misrepresentation of the classification process used in *The News Twisters* and of the content of *TNT*'s appendices.

CBS implies that *The News Twisters* has equated conservatives with "extremists of the right." No such equation has taken place.

All opinion on the right carried by CBS (and the other two networks) is grouped under the heading "conservative." Under this heading the reader will find opinion on "conservatives," "radical right," "rightists," *and* "extremists of the right." Similarly, under the heading "left," the reader will find opinion on "Yippies," "Socialist Labor Party," "Socialist Workers Party," "Communist Party," "leftists," "left-wingers," "left-wing student movement," "Cleaver's Peace and Freedom Party," "radicals," "the New Left," "SDS," *and* "extremists of the left." (See *TNT*, pages 308-310, 325-328.)

Curiously, CBS is not afflicted by the inclusion of opinion on leftist extremists under the broad heading "left." Indeed, CBS deliberately refrains from informing readers that the Humphrey attack *was* cross-indexed under anti-left opinion.

The relevant classification principle is clearly stated by *TNT* on page 251:

> When an opinion contains attack on or praise of more than one subject or issue analyzed by the study, it is classified under every heading to which it is relevant.

In accordance with this rule, the Humphrey opinion was appropriately cross-filed under anti-conservative, page 309, anti-left, page 328, and anti-black militant, page 321.

Clearly, CBS's selective indignation is spurious.

Here are summaries of the opinion coverage on conservatives carried by CBS during the period of the study—a period in which the majority of the country was supporting two conservative candidates:

Pro-Conservative: O

Anti-Conservative:

STORY NO.	SOURCE OF OPINION	
9/16/1	Candidate	Humphrey attacks extremists of the right for violence.

10/3/7 Editorial Reporter links Nixon conservatives and Wallace supporters as being the same group (racists) and for being malcontents seeking a scapegoat.

CBS does not mention or rebut these findings. Instead, it attacks the *heading* under which opinions on the right are classified.

V. War

U.S. War Policy

On the war issue, *TNT* writes:

> The opinion summaries in Appendix F reveal a steady drumbeat of anti-government voices, united in an assault on the Vietnam war. . . .
>
> [The government side] can best be described as a calculated void. . . . In general, those who might have supported the administration's side of the controversy were not to be seen or heard. There was no public opinion in support of the war on any of the three networks. There was not a word of opinion from any of the Asian nations in whose interests the war was being fought. . . . The administration's allies were, quite simply, kept off the air. (*TNT*, pages 61-64)

Here is *TNT*'s summary (page 299) of total opinion aired by CBS in favor of the U.S. war policy for the entire seven-week period of the campaign:

STORY NO.	SOURCE OF OPINION	CBS
10/9/5	Political	LBJ defends his Vietnam policy.

CBS does not mention or challenge this inconvenient finding. CBS's "spot check" skipped over it.

Bombing Halt

The major war issue during the 1968 presidential campaign was the bombing halt controversy. The government advocated a conditional bombing halt—i.e., requiring reciprocal military concessions from North Vietnam. The doves advocated an unconditional bombing halt—i.e., a unilateral suspension of bombing by the United States.

CBS gave virtually no coverage to opinion favoring the government policy—thirty-six words in all—while airing 407 words of dove opinion.

CBS does not challenge this ten to one imbalance directly. Instead, it challenges *TNT*'s classification of one opinion from Eric Sevareid—the first and most guarded of a series of progressively urgent bombing halt opinions. The entire series will be given in this section.

Opinion Number One

Herewith the accusation from the CBS study:

> *9/25/68:* This report discussed an announcement by the secretary of defense that troop strength in Vietnam would not be reduced. It concluded with the following statement which is the only reference to a bombing halt:
>
> "This interpretation of the enemy's predicament explains, at least in part, the still persisting belief that a break will come in the Paris talks. These battlefield conditions suggest that the next solid gesture toward peace may come from the enemy, but they also suggest

that another solid gesture on our part may now be appropriate and fruitful, and it is on this point that the still very real argument about stopping the bombing of North Vietnam now seems to center, inside the highest councils of this government."

Appendix F (page 304): Miss Efron classifies this as an "anti-U.S. Policy on the Bombing Halt editorial." She also cites it (page 117) as a "striking" example of a report that "claims to be presenting the arguments on both sides of a controversy—but in fact does not." Her conclusion (page 117) is that "the reporter is 'summing up' the argument within the administration over a bombing halt—and leaves out the arguments of Johnson-Rusk-Rostow and the generals."

Clearly, Miss Efron's assertion is unfounded. There is *no* "summing up" of the "argument within the administration." There is merely a reference to the existence of such an argument. *No* administration viewpoints, pro or con, are presented.

CBS Misrepresentations

This is a veritable thicket of misrepresentations of both the CBS text and *TNT*'s text. To list rapidly only the major ones:

1) CBS rewrites the beginning of its own story, leaving out the following section, the crucial context for the *TNT* analysis:
The enemy seems physically unable to seriously expand and intensify the fighting. From authoritative quarters here, the conviction here is that Hanoi has been trying for two months to mount a major offensive, but has been thrown off balance time after time by American troop mobility and *the increasing effectiveness of the bombers* and long-range artillery inside South Vietnam. (Emphasis added.)

2) CBS fails to state that *TNT*'s summary is of *covert* editorial opinion—that a particular slanting technique is involved called the Half-Debate.

3) CBS fails to cite the Half-Debate technique (*TNT*, page 117), to wit:
The reporter claims to be presenting the arguments on both sides of a controversy—but in fact, does not. *Instead, he presents the reasoning of one side very strongly—and omits the reasoning on the other side.*

4) CBS chops out the italicized and crucial half of the definition—and presents the first half as if it were *TNT*'s description of the Sevareid passage.

5) CBS stresses *TNT*'s use of the word "striking"— omitting to mention that *TNT* was describing the Sevareid passage as a "striking" use of a *covert* technique.

As for CBS's "arguments," they are best dealt with after the textual analysis of the Sevareid opinion that follows.

TEXTUAL ANALYSIS

The analysis is long—almost every sentence Sevareid utters merits scrutiny:

Sevareid summarizes reports from the secretary of defense and from General Abrams on maintaining troop strength in Vietnam, and a report from "authoritative sources" on the military success of the U.S. bombing operations. Sevareid informs us that the "increasing effectiveness" of the bombing is paralyzing the enemy.

In this context, Sevareid discusses the persistence of a "belief" that a break will come in the Paris talks. Who holds this "belief"? Only U.S. government officials have been mentioned so far, so presumably it is their "belief."

Sevareid immediately proceeds to an impersonal-sounding discussion of what these promising battle conditions "suggest," i.e., what they objectively imply, presumably to the same government observers—and to Sevareid himself.

He presents two alternative implications of these "battlefield conditions."

1) On the one hand, these battlefield conditions "suggest" that the enemy may offer a "solid gesture for peace."

2) On the other hand, these battlefield conditions "suggest" that it might be "appropriate and fruitful" for the U.S. to make a "solid gesture" for peace, i.e., to stop the bombing.

The curious thing about these alternative implications of the increasingly successful bombing tactics is that they are strictly dove alternatives. Only the doves at this time take Hanoi's peace statements seriously. And only the doves, who view the U.S. role in Vietnam as immoral, argue that it might be "appropriate and fruitful" for the U.S. to stop the bombing that has paralyzed the enemy.

These are not the alternatives implied by the battle conditions as seen by hawks, who deny that there is the slightest evidence that enemy peace feelers are sincere. The hawk view—based on the conviction that the U.S. is morally justified in this war—further holds that it is not rational to stop the bombing which is paralyzing the enemy, and that one negotiates from strength, not weakness.

But no such hawk or LBJ-Rusk-Rostow-Pentagon-type opinion is referred to here. The *language* of alternatives is used by Sevareid but the fundamental alternatives of the bombing-halt debate—the hawk vs. dove alternatives are missing. Sevareid is simply presenting the dove side of the controversy, camouflaged as a discussion of the objective implications of battle conditions.

The final camouflage of this one-sided opinion is a curious little linguistic trick. After presenting the dove idea that it is desirable for the U.S. to offer a solid gesture for peace, Sevareid says: "... and it is on *this point* that the still very real argument about the stopping the bombing of North Vietnam now seems to *center* inside the highest councils of this government." (Emphasis added.)

This notion of an argument "centered" on a "point" is odd. It has the effect of reducing the argument to a discussion of one idea—the dove proposals for a bombing halt. By this subtle formulation, Sevareid glides permanently over the existence of the other side of the argument.

In sum: Sevareid presents only the dove viewpoint—setting it in the initial context of a discussion of government plans, reports and views, and defining it in the conclusion as the focal "point" of the government argument. He thus creates the powerful illusion of reporting on a "very real argument" within the administration while presenting only one side of it.

It is for these reasons that *TNT* classifies the implicit Sevareid opinion in this passage as pro-bombing halt, and cites it as a striking illustration of the Half-Debate slanting technique.

CBS "Argument" Examined

CBS's "argument" with *TNT* can now be examined. It consists of three points:

> 1) "No administration viewpoints, pro or con, are presented."
>
> 2) "There is merely a reference to the existence of such an argument."
>
> 3) "There is *no* 'summing up' of the 'argument within the administration.' "

Here are the answers:

> 1) Administration "viewpoints" do not necessarily mean quotations from administration personnel. *TNT* refers exclusively to "arguments" within the administration. Viewpoints or arguments are *ideas*—and Sevareid *is* presenting one administration viewpoint—that of the dove (Goldberg, Harriman, Vance) contingent. He is omitting the hawk viewpoint (LBJ, Rusk, Rostow and the generals).
>
> 2) Sevareid does not simply *refer* to the existence of the argument within the administration. He *communicates* half of that argument—the pro-bombing-halt half—rapidly, fuzzily, and favorably.

3) There is assuredly *no* summing up by Sevareid of the argument within the administration. That is precisely the point *TNT* makes. What Sevareid offers is a verbal *illusion* that he is communicating the essence of the "very real argument," but it is an illusion. He is communicating only one side. It is a Half-Debate—featuring the dove position.

This is a very subtly slanted story—and the CBS "spot check" landed on this Sevareid opinion precisely because of its extreme subtlety. The combination of Sevareid's deviousness, plus a series of distortions and misrepresentations of CBS and *TNT* texts allowed CBS to pretend that Sevareid was not an active supporter of the bombing halt.

He was, however, and this was just his first opinion on the subject.

Opinion Number Two (Excluded from the CBS Study)

On 9/26—*the very next day*—Sevareid made a strong statement in favor of the bombing halt, with no camouflage at all.

He first reported on those who supported the unconditional bombing halt in Johnson's entourage and said, "Among those for it are his negotiators in Paris who are now convinced that Hanoi means just what it says, not only that nothing will happen in the direction of peace until a bombing halt, but that a bombing halt will lead to productive discussions."

And then he said (interrupted by static, yet intelligible): "There is no (...) the fact that the bombing suspension may well cost (...) American lives (...) *But this has to be weighed against the extra lives that will be lost if the war goes on and on....*" (Emphasis added.)

The italicized statement is an overt endorsement of an unconditional bombing halt by Sevareid who clearly stated that the alternative means a longer war and more deaths. The preceding context indicates that Sevareid chose to believe Hanoi's promises that unilateral military concessions by the U.S. would lead to peace.

84   HOW CBS TRIED TO KILL A BOOK

Opinion Number Three (Excluded from the CBS Study)

Before the week was out, on 10/1, Sevareid made his attitude clearer yet—by strongly, if covertly, supporting Humphrey who had just made his famous "bombing halt" speech. Sevareid said in his lead:

> In terms of his speeches, the Humphrey address of last night is clearly the most important development in the presidential campaign so far. It was a signal beamed over the head of President Johnson who was not consulted in advance, and aimed at the McCarthy-Kennedy Democrats at home and at the enemy in Hanoi. . . . The signal to Hanoi is this: Make a positive move toward peace now and negotiate an end to the slaughter with Humphrey, or take your chances with Nixon.

Sevareid here was explaining what Humphrey's "signal" "meant."

But in fact, this speech by Humphrey was startlingly and intentionally ambiguous—triggering a strong controversy among politicians and the press (including the networks) over what Humphrey really meant.

Sevareid was actually offering his own interpretation of the "signal," and "negotiate an end to the slaughter" is his own language.

The word "slaughter" applies to all wars. By those who support a war, however, it is accepted as the brutal price exacted by the cause. Americans did not refer to World War II as "the slaughter"—and hawks who see Communist aggression as a threat to human freedom do not refer to the Vietnam war as "the slaughter." This is exclusively the language of doves who consider the U.S. war in Vietnam to be immoral. Sevareid's language was the open language of a dove.

The last section of this story said:

> In the background of Humphrey's move was the concealed drama of a deeply (. . .) and divided adminis-

tration. *Several intimate and intellectual presidential advisors have joined the ranks of those convinced that a stop to the bombing of North Vietnam is the only possible way to get serious peace negotiations going and that it will have that effect (...) Demanding a (...)[1] from Hanoi in advance are Secretary Rusk, leading generals and (...) Saigon.* [Emphasis added.]

In this last passage Sevareid briefly summed up the argument within the administration over the bombing halt—and strongly, if covertly, supported the dove side.

He did it by massing "intellectuals" behind the candidate. He said that Humphrey's views were supported by a group of "intellectual" advisors to the president, who have joined "those" who believe that stopping the bombing will bring peace. Opposed to Humphrey, he said, were Secretary Rusk and leading generals— who were also LBJ advisors, but presumably not "intellectuals."

This "intellectuals" vs. "non-intellectuals" casting was a powerful glamorizing technique—to strengthen the pro-bombing-halt side of the controversy. It was also a form of name-calling or "argument from intimidation." It tacitly informed the listener that bombing-halt advocates were superior people, that hawks were inferior people, and that the listener, too, would be an intellectual inferior if he didn't agree.

Opinion Number Four (Excluded from the CBS Study)

Finally, on 10/20, Sevareid broke cover completely. In the course of making a statement on a number of other issues, he penned a quick sketch of the United States as: "... one of the world's mightiest powers, bombing and smashing one of the weakest...."

This language portraying America as a "smasher" of the weak revealed Sevareid's attitude to the war as an unmitigatedly evil act of U.S. aggression. This is the attitude which was implicit in all his prior opinion, and accounted for his systematic onesidedness.

Sevareid's advocacy of an unconditional bombing halt—explicit or implicit—was perfectly within his rights since he is a commentator. What is significant is the effort of the CBS study to conceal the fact that the CBS commentator held dove opinions—and, by implication, that he held any opinions at all.

The opinion CBS News transmitted was systematically opposed to the Vietnam war, and systematically in favor of a bombing halt. CBS prefers to conduct a war against *TNT* rather than admit it.

[1] Blurred by static, but clearly a reference to reciprocity.

VI. Anti-Nixon Opinion

The CBS "spot check" of anti-Nixon opinion—the largest body of opinion in 1968 campaign coverage—has three unusual aspects:

1) The CBS study neither mentions nor contests the strongest examples of anti-Nixon opinion cited by *TNT*.

2) The CBS executives who prepared the study released slivers of some of these strongest anti-Nixon opinions to the press—while excluding the opinion from the study.

3) The CBS study seeks to rebut only three examples out of the total body of anti-Nixon opinion, all superficially innocuous.

Illustrations of all three aspects of the "spot check" follow:

Strongest Anti-Nixon Opinion Excluded

Here, taken from *TNT*'s appendix, are my summaries of six of the longest anti-Nixon opinions by CBS reporters. These are the most sustained and most powerful expressions of anti-Nixon opinion from CBS editorial sources aired during the presidential campaign of 1968.

If CBS were as "objective" as CBS officially claims, these are the summaries the CBS study would have chosen to rebut and expose:

STORY NO.	SOURCE OF OPINION	
9/17/3	Editorial	Reporter ridicules Nixon's entry into rally; discounts crowd response as meaningless; discounts crowd response as hysterical; discounts crowd response as inevitable for Nixon's birthplace; discounts crowd response as a result of manipulation; *compares rally to football game;* says Nixon is a boring, anticlimactic presence at his own rally; criticizes Nixon as overconfident.
9/19/21	Editorial	Reporter argues with Nixon on Humphrey's behalf by reviewing a series of events in which people at home and abroad have attacked Nixon; reporter retransmits Humphrey's wisecracks at Nixon and justifies Humphrey's personal invective while discounting Nixon's political courtesy.
9/20/4	Editorial	Reporter attacks Nixon's campaign techniques; discounts repeated triumphs in city after city; discounts the convictions of Nixon's supporters and campaign contributors; discounts the significance of Nixon radio-TV statements; criticizes Nixon as devious for evading the press.
9/26/3	Editorial	Reporter discounts significance of Nixon's white middle-class youth audience; criticizes Nixon's hardcore anti-Communist past; says Nixon is appealing to race prejudice of the middle-class

young people; says Nixon is counting on race prejudice in white middle-class majority to win; suggests Nixon is a racist.

10/3/7   Editorial   Reporter links Nixon with Wallace as law-and-order racist candidate; suggests Nixon is a hypocrite, devoid of principles; says Nixon and Wallace appeal to same group of failures and malcontents.

10/24/6   Editorial   Reporter attacks Nixon on behalf of Humphrey after a strong Nixon attack on Humphrey's four-year record of failure: He says Nixon is emotionally false; that he is playing the hero; that his crowds are unenthusiastic; that he is making personal attacks on Humphrey; that he was a hard-line anti-Communist when younger who attacked the patriotism of opponents; that his campaign has a core of falsity contrived by Madison Avenue; that he pretends to be supported by youth; that his campaign promises are over-simplified and self-contradictory; *that he has not yet convinced his supporters to vote for him.*

(Emphases have been added in two stories above for the purpose of the following "sliver" analysis.)

None of these opinions by CBS newsmen were named or contested by the CBS study. The CBS "spot check" vaulted right over them.

Slivers Released to the Press

This vaulting was not accidental. CBS was very conscious of this category of extremely strong anti-Nixon opinion and handled it as follows:

- It yanked fragments of *TNT*'s summaries out of context.
- It yanked corresponding, or allegedly corresponding, fragments out of the total CBS texts.
- And it released these directly to individuals in the press as evidence of *TNT*'s bias or fraudulence.

Here are two documented cases:

Case Number One

In the September 27, 1971 issue of *Broadcasting*—two weeks before the publication date of *TNT*—an article appeared headlined "Setting the Backfires Before the Book Is Out." It was based on an interview with CBS News Vice-President David Klinger which took place half a week before, in which Mr. Klinger declared that it was "abundantly clear" that *TNT*'s analysis was filled with "an obvious bias which distorts the facts."

Within this story, the following paragraph appears:

> And when Eric Sevareid broadcast that "Mr. Nixon is hitting harder" and "stirring up the faithful just as much as he possibly can" because "he has to counteract the possible stay-at-home effects of the widespread impression that he already has it made," Mr. Klinger said, Miss Efron interpreted it as "an attack on Mr. Nixon to the effect that *'he has not yet convinced his supporters to vote for him.'*"

The emphasized fragment is recognizable: it is a sliver of one of the strong anti-Nixon opinion summaries listed above.

It is quite true that the sliver of the *TNT* summary does not correspond with the sliver of the text cited by the CBS news executive. It couldn't possibly correspond with it. The corresponding fragment of the Sevareid text is actually to be found one sentence later. It reads:

> *He must not only convince, but he must get the convinced out to the polling places.*

This sentence was not accidentally overlooked by CBS. It was the punch line of Sevareid's story. *TNT* has simply reformulated it in terms of the missing negative context.

CBS BROADCAST

Here—to illustrate what the CBS news department was *not* stressing to the press—is the full Sevareid story (10/24) followed by a detailed textual analysis.

> **Sevareid:** Richard Nixon has spent the day motorcading, grinning, and waving at the crowds through the industrial towns of Pennsylvania, a state that every winning presidential candidate has carried.
>
> He has begun to smite Humphrey, hip, thigh and thorax. . . . He says Mr. Humphrey talks too much on the delicate subject of Vietnam. Mr. Humphrey has been making attacks on Mr. Nixon's personal character for some time, but for Nixon it's a new tactic, at least so far as this campaign is concerned, but familiar to those who remember the young Nixon.
>
> His crowds are sizeable with knots, here and there, of real enthusiasm. And at the core of it all is organized spontaneity.
>
> The fingerprints of Madison Avenue are all over the operation. Usually it's a typical rally right in front of the speakers' stand. We see a rather large group of high school students with their (. . .) and their balloons. That tends to keep the hecklers at some distance from the speaker. And the kids cheer (. . .) and some drums in the distance usually roll in unison with them.
>
> Hundreds of signs appear, of course, at these rallies, most of them designed to appear handmade although they are mass produced, unless of course, every pro-Nixon family buys only red and blue paint and white (. . .) in their basement workshop.
>
> To almost any candidate the oversimplifications become even more simple as election day nears and the level of anxiety rises. So today Mr. Nixon promised 15,000,000 more jobs in the next four years, peace at

home, peace abroad, steady prices, high wages, easier taxes, but high social security payments as prices go up.

Nixon is hitting harder. He is stirring up the (. . .) faithful just as much as he can. He has to counteract the possible stay-at-home effect of the widespread impression that he already has it made. He must not only convince, but he must get the convinced out to the polling places.

TEXTUAL ANALYSIS
• Sevareid first describes Nixon as having spent the day motorcading, "grinning" and waving at the crowds.

To "grin" *(American Heritage Dictionary)* requires one "to draw back the lips and bare the teeth." To describe Nixon as spending *a whole day* "grinning" at "crowds," offering no intelligible provocation such as repeated outbursts of crowd enthusiasm, is slyly funny. The picture suggests both falsity in Nixon, and inert supporters. This latter implication is later stated explicitly by Sevareid, who denies much "real" enthusiasm in Nixon crowds.

• Sevareid next criticizes Nixon, who is attacking Humphrey. He says such personal attacks are no surprise to the people who remember the "young" Nixon.

This is common code-criticism of Nixon's character—and Sevareid also made it when Nixon wasn't attacking Humphrey. On 9/19, he said:

Both Humphrey and Nixon are trying to play new roles. Mr. Humphrey, normally a most (. . . polite[1]) public man is resorting, because he's behind, to epithets like 'Fearless Fosdick', meaning his Republican opponent. And Mr. Nixon, because he's ahead, deplores the use of even such minor epithets as that, and uses no language approaching his attacks of years ago, when he (. . . impugned[2]) the patriotism of opponents.

This reference to "the young Nixon"—like the "old Nixon" and "Tricky Dick"—is liberal code to describe Nixon's hardcore anti-communist days when he slashed savagely at liberals as communist sympathizers. It is an antagonistic reference from the liberal-left perspective.

• Sevareid now returns to his main theme: Nixon crowds, he says, show little "real" enthusiasm for him—an overtly unfavorable comment based on mass mindreading. Sevareid has not seen Mr. Nixon's crowds from coast to coast, and has no way of reading the "unreality" of their emotional enthusiasm for the candidate. This editorial opinion reinforces the same suggestion already made in the introductory sentence, when Nixon "grinned" all day . . . at nothing.

• Sevareid then makes the same point in a new way: he indicts Nixon rallies. He says that they are the "core" of the Nixon campaign, and that the "core" is "organized" or phony spontaneity contrived by "Madison Avenue." Again, he is saying: The public response to Nixon is not authentic or "real."

He cites one illustration of this alleged core of "unreality"—the practice at Nixon rallies of placing large groups of cheering high school students in front of the speakers stand where they "keep the hecklers at some distance from the speaker." Why would hecklers mobbing the candidate be more "real" than cheering students? Sevareid does not say.

He is already on record, however, with his own feeling that youthful cheers for Nixon are unbelievable. On 9/17, he says:

The presidential campaign seems to get weirder as the days go by. . . . It still seems a shock to see Hubert Humphrey, one whose passion has been the advancement of education, booed and jeered by college students. It is deeply unsettling to see Richard Nixon, unyoung, unhandsome, and unsexy, adored by female teenagers with a screaming, jumping (. . .).

• Sevareid then offers another and briefer illustration of the "unreal" spontaneity at the "core" of the Nixon "operation." It is the mass production of red-white-and-blue signs, allegedly made to look as if they were painted by hand by pro-Nixon families. Sevareid fails to mention the "real" response of the "families" who voluntarily carry and voluntarily wave these signs.

• Sevareid now criticizes Nixon again—on his "oversimplified" campaign promises, and by his choices suggests that the candidate is contradicting himself, i.e., lying to the electorate.

• And he concludes by saying that the candidate must "convince" the "convinced" to go to the polls and vote for him. The reason given: the "possible stay-at-home effect" of the view that Nixon "has it made." This ostensibly neutral remark is not neutral in a story where the reporter has already suggested *five* times that the public response to Nixon is not genuine. It is disguised reinforcement of Sevareid's central thesis that Nixon supporters do not genuinely support their candidate.

(Note: CBS aired this curious commentary with its overt and covert wallop, immediately after a Nixon attack on Humphrey's four-year record of alleged domestic and foreign failures. It functioned as an instant anti-Nixon rebuttal.)

It is from this baldly anti-Nixon story that CBS chopped out a splinter—along with an unmatched splinter from a *TNT* summary—as "evidence" for the press that *TNT* was fabricating CBS' anti-Nixon bias.

Case Number Two

On October 27, on a program on WNYC, Channel 31, called "All About TV," moderator Steven Scheuer, after heavy briefing by CBS personnel, *opened* the show with an aggressive demand that *TNT*'s author account for a certain anti-Nixon classification in *TNT*. It was an extraordinary opening question for a program on a book unknown to most of Mr. Scheuer's audience.

A CBS newsman, Mr. Scheuer began, had made the following statement in a story about a Nixon rally:

It was put together by a promoter whose usual business is staging half-time entertainment at professional football games.

TNT had classified this as an anti-Nixon opinion and, continued Mr. Scheuer, had summarized it as follows:

Reporter compares rally to football game.

Again, this fragment of a *TNT* summary will be recognized as the emphasized portion of a lengthy summary cited above.[3]
And again, this is deliberate misrepresentation.

In this case, the corresponding sentence in the CBS text *was* correctly isolated—but the surrounding context which alone made *TNT*'s interpretation possible had been chopped out.

CBS BROADCAST
Here is the reporter's narrative (9/17), followed by a textual analysis.

> **Reporter:** He had all the pomp and splendor of the entrance of the gladiators.
> A crowd of 10,000 had been warmed up for two hours with music and speeches and they responded with a special kind of hysteria not often generated for Richard Nixon.
> But this, after all, was strictly conservative Orange County, his birthplace, which Nixon has carried every time he's run for anything and will no doubt carry again.
> This rally, building to a crescendo of emotion with his triumphal entrance, was another carefully organized facet of this meticulously structured campaign.
> It is to serve as a model for other rallies yet to come, and it was put together by a promoter whose usual business is staging half-time entertainment at professional football games.
> Even the entrance seems to be an anti-climax. . . .
> Perhaps it is worth noting in this (. . .) run campaign (. . .) doing so well in the polls (. . .). One additional

measure of Nixon's confidence. He always swears (...) to what he will do in the White House after the election. It is no longer "if" but "when."

TEXTUAL ANALYSIS

● The reporter opens his story with strong sarcasm. To describe any American politician in a business suit—and the restrained Nixon in particular—as having "all the pomp and splendor ... of the gladiators" is such exaggeration as to constitute ridicule. The reporter makes this satirical intention explicit, later on: He describes this entrance of Mr. Nixon as an "anti-climax."

This ridiculing introduction is a severe undercutting of the candidate.

● The reporter then claims to divine the inner mental processes of a crowd of 10,000 people. He attributes their intense response to Nixon to the fact that they had been "warmed up for two hours with music and speeches." This suggests that the 10,000 people have been brainwashed—that their response is not an expression of their own authentic feelings towards Nixon. The reporter does not know this; it is his own opinion.

This is a *second* undercutting of the candidate by denying the meaning and value of the public response to him.

● The reporter next dismisses the intense response to Nixon as the expected reaction of people in Nixon's "birthplace"—a political loyalty of an automatic kind.

(This is "heads-I-win, tails-you-lose" selectivity. Just two days later, it suited CBS to remember that Nixon's hometown had once been hostile to him: "Protesting citizens killed a move to name a street after him, in his hometown of Whittier, all in reaction to his campaigning methods." [CBS 9/19/21, Anti-Nixon.])

The portrayal of Nixon's "birthplace" as a locus of automatic support communicates, once again, the idea of uncritical followers—a county full of them.

This is a *third* undercutting of the candidate by suggesting that the voter's response to him is unchosen, and has no value.

- The reporter then describes the "building of a crescendo of emotion" as a "carefully organized facet" of this "structured campaign." This states overtly what has already been implied—that people have been externally manipulated into this emotional response.

This is a *fourth* undercutting of the candidate, by suggesting that his supporters' emotion is engendered by external gimmicks, not by enthusiasm for him.

- The reference to the rally promoter, who also stages half-time entertainment at professional football games, is an openly sarcastic thrust. In this snide context, it suggests that there is no significant difference between the crowd's excitement at this political rally, and the crowd's excitement at a football game. Both are manufactured with "half-time entertainment."

This is a *fifth* undercutting of the candidate—again suggesting that the voter's response to him is meaningless.

- The reporter announces flatly that the entrance of Nixon "seems to be an anti-climax." To whom? Clearly not to the "hysterical" crowd. It is only an "anti-climax" to the reporter—the same reporter who has denied, in five successive paragraphs, that the crowd's emotion had any meaning. In perceiving an "anti-climax" here, the reporter reveals an inability to distinguish between external facts and his own emotions.

This is a *sixth* undercutting of the candidate—finally implying that he himself is a boring presence at his own rally.

- The story concludes with a description of the candidate as "confident"—the details clearly indicating *over*-confidence: "It is no longer 'if' but 'when.' " This is a final thrust, since over-confidence is an unattractive trait, known to boomerang in politics.

TNT SUMMARY

This is one of the half-dozen most hostile stories discovered during the period of the study. It is really not a story but a reportorial tantrum—in which the reporter sees 10,000 people wildly cheering Nixon and keeps saying: "It's not true . . . it's not true . . . it's not true."

It is from this story that the splinter about the football rally promoter was yanked by CBS—and given to the press as "evidence" that *TNT* had fabricated CBS's anti-Nixon bias.

"Safe" Stories Included

If CBS's policy was to exclude the harshest anti-Nixon opinion from the CBS study, this policy had a corollary: to include only stories on Nixon which, at least at a surface glance, appeared safe.

Three stories met that test.

Here is how CBS presented these stories to the readers of its study.

Story Number One

The CBS study says:

> *10/28/68 CBS News Transcript:* "In 1960, Richard Nixon tried to run his campaign top to bottom. This time he's found a group of smooth, intelligent, middle-class loyalists, who, like Nixon, believe in heroes, the Puritan ethic, and the American pantheon. This time he lets them work and sometimes play. The songs aboard the press plane on the electric piano soothe, they do not protest. They are more vintage Bing Crosby than Pete Seeger, and the Nixon staff is the prototype of their candidate's forgotten American. . . ."
>
> *Appendix D (page 284)* Miss Efron classifies this report as an "anti-Nixon editorial" by the reporter because "reporter describes Nixon and staff as squares who don't conform to liberal-left cultural standards; mocks their 'forgotten American' crusade."

The CBS study also says elsewhere on the page:

ANTI-NIXON OPINION

> *10/28/68 CBS News Transcript:* John Mitchell, Mr. Nixon's campaign manager describes, in a broadcast interview, the "orderly" manner in which the Republican campaign has been conducted. He concludes with this statement: "I think our operation has been, if you put it, without passion, because we have planned it and *programmed* it and have had time to carry it out." (Emphasis added.) In his "wrap-up," the reporter states: "They [the Nixon staff] understand success, and in their crusade for their oppressed majority they confidently await a programmed victory."
>
> *Appendix D (page 284)* Miss Efron classifies this as an "anti-Nixon editorial" by the reporter. Failing to note that it was Mr. Nixon's campaign manager who introduced the word "programmed" she comments that the reporter compares "Nixon and staff to inhuman computers."

This is a revealing example of the lengths to which CBS will go to disprove bias charges—by chopping up its own text, as well as *The News Twisters'* text—and by retroactively altering its text.

The first broadcast text cited by CBS is the "wrap-up" of a long piece on Nixon's campaign staff—minus the last ironic punch line.

The second broadcast text cited by CBS is the missing punch line—which CBS presents separately as the "wrap-up" of the story. CBS *does not* state that these are two parts of the same final paragraph—of the same story. Indeed, CBS *separates* them physically on the page—with a different charge against *TNT* placed between them, as though they came from two different stories.

Similarly, CBS reports that *TNT* summarizes each of these segments *independently* as different anti-Nixon "editorials."

This is willful deception. In Appendix D of *TNT*, page 284, the implicit editorial opinion of this story is thus summed up:

> *10/28/15* Reporter describes Nixon and staff as squares who don't conform to liberal-left cultural standards; mocks their "forgotten American" crusade; compares Nixon and staff to inhuman computers.

Clearly, this refers to implicit opinion from *one* editorial source, in a running sequence, and does not constitute a description of two separate "anti-Nixon editorials." (Furthermore, nowhere in *TNT* are any opinions described as "anti-Nixon [or any other kind of] editorials." What is being summarized is *implicit opinion from editorial sources.*)

What does CBS gain from chopping the conclusion of a news story into two parts and pretending that these are two separate editorial entities? One sees the advantage for CBS only from an examination of these two "editorial opinions" as presented by CBS. I analyze each here, separately.

TEXTUAL ANALYSES

The Separate Punch Line

The CBS study, once again, says:

> *10/28/68 CBS News Transcript:* John Mitchell, Mr. Nixon's campaign manager describes, in a broadcast interview, the "orderly" manner in which the Republican campaign has been conducted. He concludes with this statement: "I think our operation has been, if you put it, without passion, because we have planned it and *programmed* it and have had time to carry it out." (Emphasis added.) In his wrap-up, the reporter states: "They [the Nixon staff] understand success, and in their crusade for their oppressed majority they confidently await a programmed victory."
>
> *Appendix D (page 284)* Miss Efron classifies this as an "anti-Nixon editorial" by the reporter. Failing to note that it was Mr. Nixon's campaign manager who introduced the word "programmed" she comments that the reporter compares "Nixon and staff to inhuman computers."

CBS is determined to trace the mockery of Nixon and his staff in the final passage of the piece to Nixon campaign manager John Mitchell—not to the CBS reporter. The reporter, says CBS, is just repeating the term "programmed" first used by Mr. Mitchell.

This is something less than accurate.

John Mitchell did *not* introduce the issue of "programming" in the story—the reporter did, in describing Mitchell. In mid-story, the reporter lists the "Nixon insiders," then says:

> All of them influence policy, but none more than campaign manager John Mitchell who stays in the Park Avenue headquarters—invoking what is the watermark of this campaign—the *programming* of it all. [Emphasis added.]

The reporter then asks Mitchell a subtly offensive question about the "passionlessness" of the Nixon team. He attributes his leading question to an anonymous source:

> Another staffer has been quoted as saying that there's none of the hysteria and excitement you usually find in a political campaign—*that, in fact, you operate with absolutely no passion.* [Emphasis added.]

Mitchell's reply—uncut:

> *I don't know what passion has to do with it,* but we do operate, I believe, in an orderly fashion, and that comes from preparation. So that we have anticipated the items that will come up and the problems that will arise and we've been able to handle them in an easier-going manner than you might in an ordinary campaign when things are done at the last minute with hurry and rush, and sometimes with consternation. *I think the operation has been, as you put it, without passion because we have planned it and programmed it and have time to carry it out.* [Emphasis added.]

Having linked an absence of "passion" to the Mitchell concept of an orderly, planned, or "programmed" operation, the reporter goes one step further—he refers to Mitchell as Nixon's "programmer." A "programmer" is a term used to describe one who programs a computer. A human being cannot and does not have a "programmer" save metaphorically. This is a subtle way of describing Nixon himself, as a computer, i.e., as a machine-like man without "passion." Again the CBS reporter puts these words in someone else's mouth. He says of Herb Klein, allegedly paraphrasing him: "He [Klein] remembers that in 1960, Nixon was his own campaign manager, *had no programmer*, no John Mitchell." [Emphasis added.]

And last, the reporter completes his story with a final paragraph—the missing one—and an ironic punch line:

> They [the Nixon staff] understand success, and in their crusade for their oppressed majority, they confidently await a programmed victory.

With the prior linking of passionlessness with "programming," with the tacit description of Nixon as a "programmed" man—the emotionless-machine connotations of the term "programmed" have been fully established—by the CBS reporter, not by John Mitchell.

CBS has gone to immense trouble to deny its reporter's responsibility for the term "programmed" in this final sentence, while evading the reporter's responsibility for the dehumanizing connotations of this word. CBS has obliterated everything in the story which would explain why *TNT* says, correctly, that an *implication* of the story is that Nixon and staff are being compared to "inhuman computers."

The lengths to which CBS has gone to blot out the antecedents of this metaphor are striking. CBS appears to have altered its own text in pursuit of this goal. In the study, as released across the country, CBS shortens the Mitchell statement as follows: "I think our operation has been, *if* you put it, without passion, because we have planned it and programmed it, etc., etc."

According to our transcript, Mitchell said, "*as* you put it." According to *Broadcasting* magazine, September 27, 1971, Mitchell said, "*as* you put it."

Mitchell did say "as you put it" because he was speaking to the reporter who had just put it to Mitchell that the Nixon staff and Mitchell operated "without passion." But to grant that Mitchell was referring back to the *reporter's* charge would have interfered with CBS' determination to portray Mitchell as the originator of all references to "programming" and "programmers," to Nixon as a "programmed" being, and generally, to the offensive computer image for Nixon and a Nixon victory. So CBS changed the only word in the cut reply which shows Mitchell responding in terms *previously set* for him by his questioner.

CBS may reply, of course, that this is a typographical error. If so, be it noted that it is the only typographical error in three CBS-released documents on *TNT* and that it hits a critical word at a time when CBS profits by the error.

This effort by CBS to deliver a CBS reporter from the charge of using the emotionless-machine concept "programmed" for Nixon, the man, and for a Nixon victory seems quite futile. This particular reporter is addicted to computer analogies when talking about Nixon. On October 15, 1968, he said:

> Nearly everything Nixon does these days is *programmed*. The last three days of guarded privacy and deliberate casual moments such as this one with Jackie Gleason in Key Biscayne are moments his *programmer* has labeled (. . .) of opportunity. (Emphasis added.)

Again, the implication that Nixon is machine-like, inhuman is smuggled in—and is duly reported in the opinion summary in Appendix D of *TNT*. CBS' "spot check" somehow failed to bring this supportive item to light.

There were only two purposes to this entire absurd and dishonest maneuver—to cover the CBS reporter who had been engaged in hostile editorializing in a news story—and to impugn the credibility of *TNT*.

The Concluding Paragraph—Minus the Punch Line

The CBS study says:

> *10/28/68 CBS News Transcript:* In 1960 Richard Nixon tried to run his campaign top to bottom. This time he's found a group of smooth, intelligent, middle-class loyalists, who, like Nixon, believe in heroes, the

Puritan ethic, and the American pantheon. This time he lets them work and sometimes play. The songs aboard the press plane on the electric piano soothe, they do not protest. They are more vintage Bing Crosby than Pete Seeger, and the Nixon staff is the prototype of their candidate's forgotten American. . . .

Appendix D (page 284) Miss Efron classifies this report as an "anti-Nixon editorial" by the reporter because "reporter describes Nixon and staff as squares who don't conform to liberal-left cultural standards; mocks their 'forgotten American' crusade."

It is obvious that after CBS's scissoring has taken place, there can be no punch-line mockery over a "forgotten American crusade." The sentence containing that mockery—"*. . . in their crusade for an oppressed majority they confidently await a programmed victory*"—has been cut out by CBS. The impression is left that *TNT* simply fabricated the implication that the CBS reporter "mocks their 'forgotten American' crusade."

CBS finds it extraordinary, nonetheless, that *TNT* would sum up the bulk of this editorial opinion as an implicit description of Nixon and staff as "squares who don't conform to liberal-left cultural standards." This is a clear illustration of the degree to which CBS is culturally provincial. Here, from *TNT*'s research folders, is a section of the textual analysis that explains this summary of implicit opinion.

Nixon and his staff are described as "smooth . . . middle-class loyalists." They are said to "believe in heroes," the Puritan ethic, and the American pantheon, to prefer soothing songs to "protest" songs; to prefer Bing Crosby to Pete Seeger.

What standard of judgment determined this selection of attributes? Clearly, the "in" standards of the liberal-left subculture, which advocates the anti-heroic, sympathizes with left-wing "protest," views leftist Pete Seeger as a significant artistic figure, considers the Puritan ethic defunct, and is scornful of the American pantheon and of the "smooth" middle class. This is a subtly mocking estimate of Nixon and his staff as conservative "squares."

There is, of course, an alternative cultural perspective—that derives from the standards of the middle class itself, where the standards of judgment would include such matters as hard work, self-discipline, ambition, long-range planning, efficiency, etc. By such Horatio Alger-Protestant Ethic standards, Nixon and his staff could be lionized, rather than mocked.

The CBS reporter chooses not to use the cultural standards which would result in favorable judgments.

When one adds to all this an ironic punch line about an "oppressed majority" and a "programmed victory"—laden with the pre-set passionless-machine connotations, one does, of course, have implicit anti-Nixon, and for that matter, implicit anti-middle-class opinion.

In summary, in the CBS broadcast, this was *one* paragraph, not two. In *TNT*, this was one unbroken sequence of implicit editorial opinions—not two separate "anti-Nixon editorials." The splitting of CBS and *TNT* texts was illegitimate.

CBS's choice was to concede that this story was subtly infiltrated with anti-Nixon editorializing—or to twist the facts, improperly manipulate texts, alter language. CBS chose the latter course—to damage *TNT*.

Story Number Two

CBS's "spot check" of anti-Nixon opinion also landed on a small, innocuous little feature story. Here is one section of the story as presented by the CBS study:

> *9/25/68 CBS News Transcript:* (Concluding paragraph in a report on Mr. Nixon's campaign visit in the Seattle area): "This week's tour, all in friendly territory, is to reassure the faithful, and to boost local GOP candidates. Nixon says he is warning his staff against overconfidence, but he himself hardly looks worried."

> *Appendix D (page 281)* Miss Efron classifies this report as an "anti-Nixon editorial" by the reporter. Without setting out the actual words of the broadcast, Miss Efron writes that the CBS News reporter "says Nixon is over-confident; suggests he is a *liar*." (Emphasis added.)

Once again, this is misrepresentation:

> 1) CBS does not give the full text of this story; passages on which *TNT*'s summary are based are missing; other irrelevant passages are present.
>
> 2) CBS does not cite *TNT*'s full opinion summary, which also states that the reporter implies a "rancorous streak" in Nixon.
>
> 3) CBS fails to state that *TNT*'s summary is of *implicit* editorial opinion.

So erroneous is this presentation that one must start from the beginning to rectify it. Here are the actual passages of the CBS story on which *TNT*'s anti-Nixon classification was based:

> **Reporter:** ... as the candidate posed at the bow, he who dislikes hats of any kind was offered a hard hat for the shipyard visit.
>
> **Nixon:** My God, I'm not going to wear that hat.
>
> **Man:** It's up to you.
>
> **Reporter:** *But it was a regulation, so at the last minute he did put it on, a little grudgingly perhaps, after telling newsmen it was the last time they'd see him in a hat during the campaign....*
>
> **Nixon:** All right, here we go! Fire!

Reporter: *Nixon says he keeps warning his staff against overconfidence, but he himself hardly looks worried.*

The implications of these selected passages of this little CBS story are subliminal—yet clearly negative:

- Faced with Nixon's disinclination to wear a hard hat, the reporter could have used such neutral words as "unwillingly," or "reluctantly," or "resistantly" or "unenthusiastically." Or he could have used more colorful, but good-tempered words like "grumblingly." Or he could even have said that Nixon "groused" about it. Instead the reporter chose the negative word "grudgingly"—"grudge" being a word that has among its primary definitions the concepts of *resentment* and *rancor (American Heritage Dictionary).*
- The reporter—in an otherwise vacuous passage—then uses the "He-says-one-thing-but-he-looks-another" structure—a classic device to alert a listener to self-contradiction, i.e., to falsity. He says that Nixon *"says"* he is alerting his staff to the dangers of overconfidence, but that Nixon doesn't *"look"* as if he is worried. The double implication is that he really feels that overconfidence is no danger (which suggests that he is overconfident), and that Nixon is not telling the truth, i.e., that he is lying.

This is a technically interesting little story, because in two swift formulations, the reporter weaves in, subliminally, two elements of a recognizable anti-Nixon stereotype: *Grudge-bearing Tricky Dick.* It is precisely by such subliminal means that political stereotypes, favorable and unfavorable, are propagated and sustained in the media.

It is interesting to note, by contrast, how a CBS reporter, in an equally vacuous little story, characterizes Hubert Humphrey. Here is the story:

Reporter: *10/25/4* Humphrey's last few stops in Los Angeles were of the traditional political stunt variety, a visit to a delicatessen where he purchased two cheddar cheese bagels and sniffed somewhat hesitantly at a plate of lox and onions. The vice-president leaves California today after some heavy campaigning, mostly among minority groups whose votes have to go to him overwhelmingly to give him any chance at all to carry this state.

Identically the same two elements exist in this Humphrey situation as in the Nixon situation: Both candidates are engaged in vote-getting maneuvers. And both show resistance to some minor activity—wearing a hard hat, and eating a plate of lox and onions.

Humphrey's resistance, however, is described with the word "hesitantly," not with the word "grudgingly." There is no implication whatever of resentment or any other unattractive emotion. On the contrary, the picture of Humphrey is winning. He sniffs hesitantly, like a puppy, at unfamiliar food. Indeed, his hesitancy clearly implies that Humphrey is not crazy about the "political stunt" in which he is engaged, that he is being pushed into it by circumstances beyond his control—by political "tradition."

Thus, a subliminally sympathetic portrait emerges—of an honest man who is forced by political necessity to do things he doesn't like to do.

At no point, in this little story, does the editorial narrative imply any phoniness or falsity in Humphrey—even in the middle of a crude ploy involving the televised consumption of Jewish food to gain votes.

Words have their own unique power, and it is not coincidental that in CBS News, 1968, Humphrey sniffs "hesitantly" while Nixon puts on a hat "grudgingly"; that Humphrey is somehow obligated by "tradition" to engage in phony political maneuvers, while Nixon talks-one-way-but-looks-another. One is Honest Hubert—the other is Grudging Tricky Dick. One is all heart. From the other, one dare not buy a used car. Reporters who think in stereotypes will reproduce these stereotypes even on the minutest of canvases.

CBS affected shock at the *TNT* summary which stated that a CBS reporter suggested that Nixon was a *liar*. Such hints and charges that Nixon was a liar, or was telling specific lies, were all over the airwaves in 1968, both in covert and overt form, from reporters and politicians. One example of a covert charge by a CBS reporter has already been cited. On 10/24, Eric Sevareid ironically lists apparently contradictory campaign promises of Mr. Nixon, implying that he is lying to the electorate (page 91 of this report). Further:

> On 9/30, Humphrey charged that Nixon did not tell the truth.
> On 10/25, Humphrey charged that Nixon did not tell the truth.
> On 9/30, Wallace charged that Nixon did not tell the truth.
> On 10/23, Wallace charged that Nixon did not tell the truth.
> On 10/16, Ramsey Clark charged Nixon with deliberately misleading.
> On 10/25, Clark Clifford challenged Nixon's veracity.
> On 10/25, Lawrence O'Brien charged Nixon with making vicious and false accusations.

In fact, CBS carried as many politicians' charges that Nixon was lying as both of the other networks put together, and twice as many as NBC.[4]

There is no reason for CBS, in particular, to be shocked by the word *liar*, applied to Nixon.

Story Number Three

In 1968, CBS commentator Sevareid repeatedly commented on candidate Humphrey and candidate Nixon and repeatedly compared them in his campaign stories. *TNT* often classifies such opinion as pro-Humphrey and anti-Nixon, and says (page 128): "80 percent of the pro-Humphrey opinion comes from one reporter, stationed primarily in one city, who ran a Humphrey campaign of his own on the air." This reporter was Eric Sevareid.

The CBS study neither acknowledges nor contests this finding. Its "spot check" leaps lightly over all such Sevareid stories which deal exclusively with Nixon, or Nixon in contrast to Humphrey. It lands instead on an ostentatiously neutral commentary in which Sevareid appears to be criticizing *all three* presidential candidates.

The CBS study reproduces the Sevareid story (10/2) as follows:

> *CBS News Transcript:* "Reason itself is bruised every day. Each of the three candidates implies that as president he would drastically reduce crime, even though crime is essentially a local problem, governors having more authority in the matter than presidents. And criminals are no respecters of political parties. The facts, which have no significance at all save to illustrate the point, are that the four states with more than 2,000 serious crimes per year per hundred thousand people, are all run by Republican governors, and in murder and manslaughter taken separately, Mr. Wallace's state of Alabama leads the nation. Humorless politics can be dangerous politics, if only because of the inevitable rude awakenings. Candidate Nixon tells us he will sweep the streets of Washington clear of prowlers and muggers. Candidate Humphrey tells us he would put an end to poverty in America. He will do in four years to eight years, in other words, what centuries of human efforts could not do. It must have been in the middle of a political campaign that a British statesman of long ago remarked 'Between craft and credulity, the voice of reason [is] stifled.'"

Then the CBS study continues:

> *Appendix D (page 282):* Miss Efron sees in this an "anti-Nixon editorial" by the reporter because "reporter links Nixon with Wallace as law-and-order racist candidate, in contrast to over-generous humanitarian Humphrey." The meaning of this report is clear. The reporter was citing one example for each of the three major candidates to illustrate how "reason itself is bruised" by the candidates during the campaign. Miss

Efron ignores the point made by the report, i.e., that Mr. Humphrey's promise to end poverty was completely unrealistic and "bruised reason." There is no basis for the charge that Mr. Nixon and Mr. Wallace are described as "racist" candidates.

This, once again, is misrepresentation.

- CBS renders *TNT*'s analysis unintelligible by failing to state that *TNT* is summarizing covert opinion in this story.
- CBS suppresses *TNT*'s more detailed analysis of the covert dimension of this Sevareid story; it appears in the chapter on covert slanting techniques (page 115):

Fake Neutrality
There is yet another category of editorializing which may be described as "Fake Neutrality." It consists of a calculated effort to make the reporter appear neutral when in fact he is taking sides. . . .

False Series
This technique was evoked on CBS alone and appears to be the invention of a particular reporter. It is a violation of a basic rule of logical categorizing, taught to children on the well-known children's show "Sesame Street" by means of a little refrain: "One of these things is not like the other." The reporter creates an ostensibly logical series in which "one of the things is not like the other." To cite one example: The reporter indicates with great precision that he intends to present a series of criticisms of all three presidential candidates on certain grounds. He explains the grounds. He then cites an illustration of Mr. Wallace's errors in this matter. He follows by an illustration of Mr. Nixon's errors in this matter. But when it's time to get to Mr. Humphrey's errors in this matter, the reporter . . . changes the subject. (CBS 10/2/18, Anti-Nixon.)

By suppressing this information, CBS prevents the reader of the CBS study from discovering that he must look for a promised, logical series which breaks in midstream, and that he must search for the covert meaning of that break.

TEXTUAL ANALYSIS

* Sevareid opens with a criticism applicable to "each of the three candidates" on the subject of their crime, or law-and-order, positions. He proceeds to present arguments against the allegedly unrealistic law-and-order positions of the first candidate, Wallace, then against the second candidate, Nixon, citing explicit examples, in each case, of their "unrealism." When the time comes for explicit criticism of the third candidate, Mr. Humphrey—the crime series stops abruptly, and the reporter changes the theme.

* Sevareid now deals with Humphrey separately in a way which covertly boomerangs at Nixon. He chides Humphrey for unrealistically pledging to "put an end to poverty in America." This has the effect of contrasting Mr. Humphrey's "guilt" of being "unrealistically" humanitarian with the "guilt" of law-and-order candidates, Nixon and Wallace, of being "unrealistically" punitive.

It is a spurious criticism of Humphrey, in that pledges by presidential condidates to "end poverty in America" are not considered flaws of unrealism—but, indeed, are considered politically mandatory. Sevareid, himself, on 10/22, says, "There is a weird *unreality* about hunger and deprivation in the middle of enormous wealth . . ." signifying that he, too, does not see this poverty as necessary.

* Finally, since one of the punitive law-and-order candidates is Mr. Wallace (a known antagonist to blacks), and since Mr. Nixon is specifically criticized by the reporter for promising to "sweep the streets clear" of "prowlers" and "muggers" in Washington, D.C. (statistically blacks), Humphrey's oversized commitment to the poor (mainly blacks) carries with it the

covert suggestion that Humphrey, alone, of the three is not a racist. This undercuts the criticism of Humphrey—and transmits a severe tacit criticism of Nixon.

• Sevareid's covert suggestion of Nixon's racism is reinforced by the fact that in liberal-left circles, the hue and cry about crime, and law and order is declared to be code for race prejudice. And it is further reinforced by the omission of Humphrey's own pledges to fight crime, and his violent attacks against black extremists who "terrorize" America. (See page 19 f. of this report for one example.)

Sevareid *could* have included evidence of Humphrey's anti-crime "unrealism" and presented the three candidates in tandem, as promised. He deliberately chose not to. It was this choice, above all, which, by *default*, tied Nixon to Wallace. The ruptured logical series was the crucial *means* of creating this tie.

Other Nixon-Wallace Links (Not Included in the CBS Study)

The linking of Nixon and Wallace was not restricted, on CBS, to this one heavily camouflaged version by Sevareid. On the very next day, another CBS reporter made Sevareid's point far more strongly. Here is just one passage from this story:

Reporter: Nixon has so far tried to offer a contrast in style not a confrontation of beliefs with Wallace. Senator Thurmond once said Nixon's stand on law and order was similar to Wallace's. Nixon declined an opportunity to repudiate that.

Here again is the identical implication. Obviously no candidate was required to "repudiate" a true law-and-order position, i.e., an opposition to crime and violence. The only thing to be repudiated was any Wallaceite or *racist* motivation behind the law-and-order position. By saying that "Nixon declined . . . to repudiate" the Thurmond statement, the CBS reporter is saying that it was the *racist* motivation for law and order which Nixon had declined to repudiate. This is to suggest that Nixon is a racist.

Again on 10/14, a CBS reporter implied that Agnew, Nixon's representative to the South, was a racist who held forth on the "Wallace themes" of law and order (see page 22 of this report).

This, too, is what Sevareid was intimating—the notion that the anti-crime or law-and-order position was a "Wallace theme" shared by the Republican candidate.

CBS preferred to evade such obvious editorial linkings of Nixon and Wallace in its news stories, to screen them out of the CBS study and to stand pat on Sevareid's version concealed under a facade of ostentatious neutrality.

NBC Joins CBS

Although CBS is the only one of three networks to undertake a full-scale campaign against *TNT*, NBC, on at least one occasion, joined CBS in feeding alleged evidence of *TNT* distortion to the press—specifically to Roger Tatarian, UPI vice-president and editor.

Mr. Tatarian's subsequent attack on *TNT* appeared in his column of October 28, and was sent to UPI papers all over the nation. The full Tatarian story appears in Appendix E of this report.

In his story, Mr. Tatarian charges that *TNT*'s findings are based on a series of distortions. He backs up this charge with two illustrations taken from the CBS study. (See references in the Preface, page xxxvii.) Both have already been demonstrated, in this report, to be riddled with CBS misrepresentation.

The third and most important illustration of *TNT*'s alleged distortion is an NBC story on an early Nixon visit to Philadelphia. NBC, says Mr. Tatarian, has given him "the full text" of the story and he prints it:

Here is what Mr. Tatarian writes:

> On page 285, [Miss Efron] portrays an NBC broadcast of September 20, 1968, in these words: "Reporter suppresses intensity of Nixon's triumph in Democratic

Philadelphia as reported by two other networks, and devotes the whole story to 'proving' that it was not a success at all, that the crowds were not for Nixon."

When you get the full text from NBC, this is what you find:

Brinkley: Chet Huntley is off tonight. I'm David Brinkley, NBC News.
 When a candidate campaigns downtown in a big city . . . it is wise to arrive during the lunch hour . . . to catch the maximum number of people on the streets . . . whether they came out to see him or not.
 Vice-President Humphrey rode through Philadelphia at mid-day two weeks ago . . . and Richard Nixon was there at mid-day today.
 The city generally is Democratic . . . but those who saw both candidates there say—for whatever it may prove—that Nixon's crowd was bigger.
 In any case . . . Nixon's turnout was large . . . and here's a report from NBC News correspondent Herbert Kaplow.

Kaplow: Nixon came here knowing that his opponent didn't get much of a reception here a week or so ago—Nixon was determined to do better, and apparently has. So, this is more fuel for Nixon's fast start.
 His campaign is diverse, as we saw during this past week. Not only did he move into an urban center such as Philadelphia—there were visits to smaller, and different type communities—Salt Lake City; Fresno, California; Springfield, Missouri; and Peoria, Illinois.
 It was the kind of political situation Nixon likes—technically, he was in the enemy camp—but it was a weak enemy—and so he rode through downtown Philadelphia looking more like the hero, than the man who technically should've been the hero, Hubert Humphrey.

This is *not* the full text of the NBC story—nor does the summary sentence from *TNT* apply to the total text; it applies to implicit editorial opinion included in the story. *TNT* does not summarize "stories" at all, only pro and con opinion in stories.

Significantly, NBC's "full text" does not include four of eight passages chosen by *TNT* as vehicles of implicit anti-Nixon editorializing. (And, unexplainably, the order of several of the editorial-narrative passages is not the order that appears in *TNT*'s transcripts.)

NBC Broadcast

Here are the precise passages from *TNT* research which explain the summary of implicit editorial opinion. They are followed by a textual analysis. (Phrases are emphasized to make the textual analysis easier to follow.)

> When a candidate campaigns downtown in a big city, it is always wise to get there during lunch hour to catch the maximum number of people on the streets, *whether they came out to see him or not.*
>
> Vice-President Humphrey rode through Philadelphia at mid-day two weeks ago and Richard Nixon was there today at mid-day. The city is generally Democratic, but those who saw both candidates say, *for whatever it may prove,* that Nixon's crowd was bigger.
>
> It is the kind of political situation Nixon wants (. . .) Nixon rode through downtown Philadelphia *looking more like the hero than the man who technically should have been the hero, Hubert Humphrey.*
>
> Pennsylvania has twenty-nine electoral votes, the third largest block. Nixon wants it. And today it *appeared* he might get it, *despite an occasional sign of disapproval.* . . .
>
> Nixon came here knowing his opponent didn't get much of a reception here a week and a half ago. Nixon was determined to do better and *apparently* he has. *His organization came through.*
>
> In (. . .) virtually everywhere, he talked about the silent solid majority, the forgotten Americans who must be listened to also. . . . The people have been responding

to Richard Nixon. As he and his wife move about the country they are being accepted as a familiar pair of visitors which, at this time, seems to be a political asset. They are projecting the image of stability and in this turbulent year, that may be the deciding political asset. *That's what Nixon's counting on, anyway.*

TEXTUAL ANALYSIS

NBC's reporters subtly slant this news story against Nixon by means of suppression and undercutting devices.

Suppression is the basis of this story—without which the other slanting methods could not be used. What is being suppressed is the intensity of the enthusiasm of the Philadelphians for Nixon.

Here are two descriptions of this phenomenon, as reported by ABC and CBS:

> *ABC: 9/20, Pro-Nixon:* "The motorcade was suddenly enveloped in a blizzard of confetti and ticker tape. The crowd deepened on both sides of the route and the sidewalks were jammed, and Richard Nixon came alive. The crowd was significantly larger and more enthusiastic than the one that greeted Hubert Humphrey just eleven days ago."
>
> *CBS: 9/20, Pro-Nixon:* "By all counts, this (...) reception is far bigger and more enthusiastic than what Philadelphia gave Hubert Humphrey."

Only in contrast to this, can one judge the NBC story.

The NBC reporters use a series of anti-climactic undercutting devices to diminish the significance of this event:

- Reporter One introduces his story by pointing out that the maximum number of people are on the streets at lunch hour, and may or may not be there to see the candidate. This suggests immediately that the size of the crowd greeting Nixon is accidental or random, and cannot be credited to his political appeal.
- He informs us that those who saw both candidates say, "for whatever it may prove" that Nixon's crowd was "bigger." He thus suppresses the issue of crowd

enthusiasm altogether, and, for the second time suggests that the size of the crowd may mean nothing.

- Reporter Two then says that Nixon rode through downtown Philadelphia "looking more like the hero than the man who technically should have been the hero." By this curious formulation, Humphrey's "heroism" would have been authentic, but Nixon's simply "looks like" it. Again, for the third time, the reporter introduces the notion of an illusion: Nixon may not be the "hero" at all.
- Next, Reporter Two informs us that Nixon wants Pennsylvania's twenty-nine electoral votes—and that "it appeared he might get it." Once again, there is the suggestion that the triumph may be illusory, followed by a quick, undercutting reference to "an occasional sign of disapproval."
- After this, Reporter Two tells us again that Nixon was determined to do better in Philadelphia, and "apparently" he had—yet another suggestion that the triumph might be ephemeral.
- Reporter Two then undercuts once again. He informs us that all this was a matter of "organization"—i.e., that Nixon has good advance men. This is yet another suggestion that the crowds are not there out of any genuine response to the candidate.
- By now, the Nixon triumph has been undercut on six separate occasions. Reporter Two mentions that virtually everywhere Nixon goes, he talks about "the silent solid majority," the "forgotten American who must be listened to also."

And, buried within the reporter's conclusion, is the statement of what the reporter has been consistently resisting since the first line of the story—namely, that "the people have been responding to Nixon."

- But he concedes this, apparently, in order to give a *psychological* reason for this national "response": Mr. and Mrs. Nixon, he says, offer an "image of stability" to the public—and that is what "Nixon is counting on, anyway."

To arrive at this psychological analysis, the reporter has presumably read the American public's "mind," and discovered a craving for an "image of stability" in the White House. And he has presumably read Nixon's mind, and discovered that Nixon, too, has read the public's mind, and is now "counting" on this telepathic insight to move him into the White House.

In fact, the reporter has read no minds, does not know what psychological desires motivate all Nixon supporters, and does not know that Nixon is "counting" on this extreme overgeneralization at all. This is the reporter's amateur psychoanalysis, and all his own opinion.

By virtue of what he is suppressing, it is anti-Nixon opinion. The reporter is suppressing a *political* interpretation of the Nixon sweep. He is failing to give the side of the story as the "silent solid majority" sees it—namely, he is suppressing all information pertaining to their antagonism to, and loss of confidence in, the Democrats and liberals and their left-wing contingent.

This is consequently a politically one-sided interpretation, sheltering the Democrats and liberals, and failing to grant that Nixon has serious political power behind him. The reporter substitutes amateur psychology for the recognition of Nixon's political potency: He presents Nixon as dull therapy for shattered nerves—and not as a political leader.

This is the ultimate undercutting of Nixon—the eighth in one story reporting on what ABC and CBS describe as a tremendously successful political event. NBC communicates the information that Nixon has done well in Philadelphia, but the undercutting by the reporters is so consistent, the anticlimactic technique is so repetitive, that one may charge the editorial narrative with being shot through with implicit anti-Nixon opinion.

NBC, like CBS, is seriously irresponsible in regard to distributing loose charges of *TNT* distortions to the press. The distribution of partial texts labeled as full texts, and the mysterious exclusion of *half* the passages which carry tacit undercuttings of Nixon's Philadelphia triumph result in serious misrepresentation both of the network's own coverage, and of *TNT*'s analytical methods.

In the case of this particular story, it was also logically obligatory upon NBC (and UPI) to compare the NBC stories with ABC and CBS stories, since *TNT*'s summary clearly states: "Reporter suppresses intensity of Nixon's triumph in Democratic Philadelphia *as reported by two other networks*. . . ."

When a network news story is slanted by means of suppression or omission techniques, the resultant slanting of the copy is not self-evident. It requires a comparison of texts—often of the coverage of three networks—to make the reader aware of the missing information or of how the same information could have been presented differently.

Despite the clear warning that this was precisely such a story, both NBC, and its outlet UPI, evaded this fact.

This then, setting NBC aside, is how the CBS study dealt with the outstanding political charge in *TNT*—that CBS had slanted opinion against Nixon by 16:1.

CBS' alleged "spot check" resulted in:

- Systematic omission from the CBS study of the strongest and most hostile examples of anti-Nixon editorializing.
- Dissemination to the press of innocuous snippets selected from these most hostile examples, combined with active misrepresentations of the CBS texts, and *TNT* analyses.
- Selection of only three superficially "safe" anti-Nixon opinions for challenge, and sheltering these with a complex series of misrepresentations, omissions, and outright falsifications.

CBS has refuted *nothing* in the anti-Nixon realm. One cannot refute analyses that one refuses to name, present, and discuss.

[1,2] Static blurred these words. The sense of the passage, however, is unmistakable.

³This same fragment was part of the repertoire of former CBS documentary producer Andrew Rooney, who represented the network side in a debate with *TNT*'s author on "Firing Line" filmed on September 1, 1971—six weeks before *TNT* publication date. He cited it as evidence of *TNT* distortion in a postmortem following the filming.

⁴See *TNT*, Appendix D.
    ABC: Humphrey 9/20/3, 10/7/4, 10/25/7; Clifford 10/25/6
    NBC: Humphrey 10/21/4; Wallace 10/24/8; Clifford 10/25/3

VII. Democratic Party Dominance

TNT charges the networks with systematic bias in favor of the Democratic party as opposed to the Republican party during the last seven weeks of the presidential campaign of 1968.

The CBS study answers this charge with the "spot check" technique, alighting on:

1) An alleged statistical discrepancy in the case of Wallace.

2) A statistical argument in the case of Nixon.

3) An alleged statistical discrepancy in the case of Humphrey.

Each is examined in turn.

Wallace and the Dominant Democrats

The CBS study says:

Miss Efron states at the conclusion of her discussion of news coverage of George Wallace (page 61): *"The coverage of opinion of George Wallace is heavily weighted against Wallace."* Yet her chart (page 36) shows that CBS broadcast 1079 words for Wallace and 1282 words against him. [Emphasis added.]

This is a misrepresentation of the section called "Candidate Wallace" (pages 56 to 61). This section makes the charge that the pattern of coverage reflects the perspective of the Democratic party, and consists largely of four elements (*TNT*, page 56):

1) Quotations from union men who were for Wallace.

2) Quotations from Democratic party and union leaders who are appalled by the falling away of this Democratic vote to Wallace.

3) Violent indictments of Wallace by the Democratic establishment, with a little assistance from reporters.

4) Reports on verbal and physical assaults on Wallace [the violence tacitly sanctioned by network men].

TNT SUMMARY
In sum: *the coverage of opinion on George Wallace is heavily weighted against Wallace* and editorially sanctions the physical attacks upon him. Editorial choices were repeatedly made to render the anti-Wallace side of the controversy more "forceful." [Emphasis added.]

This is the context from which the CBS quotation from *TNT*—the emphasized segment—was ripped, and presented as though it were a quantitative statement. But the section called "Candidate Wallace" is *not* quantitative. The *TNT* charge is qualitative—namely, that the content of opinion transmitted on Wallace reflected the *perspective* and *interests* of the Democratic Party. One cannot rebut a qualitative analysis with word counts.

Nixon and the Missing Republicans

The CBS "spot check" does not land on any pro-Nixon opinion—for good reason. There is almost none to land on. Here are the quantitative findings, for all three networks:

	PRO-NIXON	ANTI-NIXON
ABC	869	7493
CBS	320	5300
NBC	431	4234

Here, taken from *TNT*, are the summaries of all opinions favorable to Nixon carried by CBS News:

STORY NO.	SOURCE OF OPINION	
9/17/3	Public	Crowd supports Nixon in hometown.
9/18/8	Public	Nixon supporters drown out hecklers.
9/19/3	Public	Crowd supports Nixon.
	Editorial	Reporter praises Nixon for "staying on the high road" in his attack on Democratic administration.
	Public	Young admirer throws roses at Nixon.
9/20/4	Public	Crowd supports Nixon.
9/30/4	Public	Crowd supports Nixon.
10/3/7	Public	Crowd supports Nixon.
	Public	Crowd supports Nixon.
10/18/1	Editorial	Reporter sympathetically describes Nixon's "good-natured jabs" at his opponent.
10/28/10	Political	Eisenhower and wife support Nixon.
10/28/15	Political	Nixon assistant, Pat Buchanan, expresses confidence that Nixon will launch the country in new direction, start solving problems of the cities.

Political	Nixon assistant, Raymond Price, is intensely loyal to Nixon.
Political	Nixon assistant, Price, says Nixon is a man of great dimensions.

Note the absence of public opinion favorable to Nixon—a curious absence given the fact that during most of the campaign period he had a commanding lead in the polls.

Note, also, the absence of support for Nixon from Republicans. The only Republicans cited as supporting or approving of him are the late President Eisenhower and his wife (about to become Nixon in-laws), and two Nixon staff members, Pat Buchanan and Raymond Price.

What is missing from this canvas of opinion, as presented by CBS newsmen is: the American public and the Republican party.

CBS comments on these findings in only one short section of its ten-page study—thrown in at the bottom of page 9. CBS argues:

> Miss Efron states (page 32) that, during the study period of seven weeks on which her conclusions are based, there were only 320 "words spoken for" Mr. Nixon on the CBS "Evening News." A quick check of the broadcast transcripts shows that, during the period in question, the CBS "Evening News" carried a total of 4747 words spoken *only by Mr. Nixon* in the course of his campaign—and presumably spoken in his own behalf as a candidate. But this fact does not appear in the book. Certainly, it is pertinent to an evaluation of the coverage given to Mr. Nixon.

This is nonsensical criticism:

1) CBS is simply complaining that *TNT* has done a pro-and-con opinion study, not some other kind of study.

2) CBS is demanding that a candidate's words be interpreted in terms of *motive*, not of *meaning*.

The CBS News Department ignored the pro-Nixon attitudes of the Republican party and its public supporters during the presidential campaign of 1968. No rearrangement of the material can compensate for seven weeks of coverage in which the only political figures of his own party to praise Nixon on the CBS-controlled air waves were Dwight and Mamie Eisenhower, Pat Buchanan and Raymond Price.[1]

Humphrey and the Democratic Alliance

The CBS "spot check" does not land on pro-Humphrey opinion. Its amount is embarrassing, as compared to the amount granted to Nixon.

CBS instead resorts to the same device already used in the Wallace section: It pits a verbal fragment from a qualitative analysis against word totals—and tries to claim a contradiction; to wit (CBS study, Appendix B, page 146):

> Miss Efron states (page 55) that the networks actively favored Hubert Humphrey and portrayed him as a *"saint studded over with every virtue known to man."* Yet her chart (page 33) shows that CBS broadcast 2388 words for Humphrey, only slightly more than the 2083 words spoken against Humphrey. [Emphasis added.]

The section of *TNT* which CBS is discussing is entitled "Candidates Humphrey and Nixon." It compares the opinion selectivity of all three networks on both candidates, detailing in five pages, the praise and criticism accorded only to their *characters.*

On page 55, the conclusion of this qualitative comparison says:

> It should now be said that none of these opinions include the views of opposing candidates. Neither Mr. Nixon's criticisms of Mr. Humphrey nor Mr. Humphrey's criticisms of Mr. Nixon are included in this array of alleged character attributes. Nor do these lists include

public opinion or the running daily praise and attack on a variety of purely political issues. This contrasting portrait of the characters of Richard Nixon and of Hubert Humphrey is exclusively the result of the combined opinions of politicians and reporters.

Network reporters in alliance with Democratic-liberal politicians portrayed Hubert Humphrey as a talkative Democratic *saint studded over with every virtue known to man.* Deprived of reporters in league with Republican-conservative politicians, Mr. Nixon is not portrayed as a human being at all but is transmogrified into a demon out of the liberal id.

Given this loading of the political decks, there is no need to analyze the other types of pro and con opinion on Messrs. Nixon and Humphrey. The opinion in Appendix D is worth reading—particularly the one-sided editorial assault on Nixon as an evader of the issues, while Mr. Humphrey, whose ambiguities merited a similar charge, is spared. But when an assault of this magnitude is directed at the most crucial aspects of a human being and presidential candidate—his mind, his morality and his character—nothing else is of much significance.

The emphasized phrase is the quotation CBS yanks from this context—and seeks to pit against word totals on Humphrey alone.

What is at stake here, however, is not the amount of general pro and con opinion on Humphrey, but *sources of opinion and internal patterns of coverage on the characters of both candidates:* a reporter-Democratic party alliance praising Humphrey on the one hand—and no reporter-Republican alliance to balance it.

CBS resorts to this device because there is no way for it to deny the existence of Democratic party dominance in its campaign coverage of 1968.

[1] This reliance by CBS on Nixon "speaking in his own behalf" reappeared six months later (and after I had written this section) as an important theme in the CBS-commissioned INRA study (see Preface). This gives one an idea of how INRA discovered so many "references" favorable to Nixon, despite INRA's own findings of an extreme shortage of Republican and pro-Republican sources.

VIII. Liberals vs. The News Twisters

The News Twisters leads to one broad conclusion—that the tri-network pattern of political bias is left-liberal. On page 47, the general conclusions are thus stated:

> The actual amounts of opinion on each issue vary considerably from network to network and the degree of bias, and sometimes its direction, shifts both from network to network, and from issue to issue. The picture is not consistent.
>
> But the preponderant opinion slant is unmistakable. Based on these figures alone, one can make these statements about this period of coverage:
>
> ● The networks actively slanted their opinion coverage against U.S. policy on the Vietnam war.
> ● The networks actively slanted their opinion coverage in favor of the black militants and against the white middle-class majority.
> ● The networks largely evaded the issue of violent radicals.
> ● The networks actively favored the Democratic candidate, Hubert Humphrey, for the presidency over his Republican opponent.

- The networks actively opposed the Republican candidate, Richard Nixon, in his run for the presidency.

The CBS study argues that *TNT* cannot, on the basis of these findings, conclude "that network coverage tends to be strongly biased in favor of the liberal-left axis of opinion." CBS's reason: ". . . according to her chart (page 40), CBS broadcast 120 words *against* liberals, and *not one word* for liberals."

"This," says CBS, "illustrates strikingly the invalidity of her statistical approach."

CBS is mistaken. This illustrates strikingly CBS's commitment to equivocation.

In the study period, CBS newscasts carry little opinion on liberals per se—liberal news agencies unlike conservative and radical agencies, tending not to see liberalism as an object of critical investigation and controversy. This failure to cover the unstated axioms of the CBS news department scarcely invalidates the total constellation of opinion on the whole group of thirteen subjects studied, which adds up, both quantitatively and qualitatively, to a clear-cut Democratic-liberal-left pattern. The opinions selected and stressed by network reporters on these subjects were almost invariably the opinions voiced by the left-liberals in 1968.

TNT, for that matter, addresses itself to the apparent contradiction on which CBS has seized. Pages 64 to 67 of *TNT* explain exactly why, despite the figures cited by CBS, virtually all opinion on liberals and conservatives carried on all three networks is *favorable* to liberals. On all three networks, only conservatives are portrayed as racists. This casts liberals, explicitly or by default, as morally transcendent on this issue. Indeed, CBS's only "anti-liberal" opinion in seven weeks (10/21) came from George Wallace, a known racist. As *TNT* comments, "Statistics notwithstanding, there is no contradiction here of the network bias pattern."

CBS is pretending to "refute" 350 pages of documentation with this little statistical paradox—identified and explained by *TNT* itself.

If all of *The News Twisters* could be refuted so "strikingly" with this single little statistic, one wonders why CBS bothered to write its study at all.

IX. Conclusion

You have now seen the nature of CBS News President Richard Salant's chief "intellectual" weapon against *The News Twisters*. Its lack of integrity should be apparent.

It was intended to expose the alleged corruption at the base of *TNT*. But it is precisely that base which the CBS study evaded, misrepresented and falsified.

Social scientists who have supported *The News Twisters* made three cardinal points about the CBS study. They have already been quoted at length and I summarize them here:

1) According to Professor Paul H. Weaver of Harvard University: CBS's sampling of items is statistically insignificant.

2) According to Professor David Haight of Hunter College: CBS is challenging a dispensable element of *The News Twisters*. When covert editorializing by reporters is removed, leaving intact the bulk of overt opinion from others, the bias pattern remains the same.

3) According to Dr. George Weinberg, author of *Statistics: An Intuitive Approach:* To dispute *TNT*'s research

without having examined that research is morally derelict: "What could be lower than that on the scale of human decency?"

These three statements capture what is so essentially spurious about the CBS study and each merits a little elaboration.

Professor Weaver's comment tells you that the CBS study cannot be viewed even remotely as a rebuttal or refutation of *The News Twisters*, since it deals with only nine opinions—a microscopic portion of the 300,000 words that were analyzed. In any content analysis, there is room for a disagreement factor of some 30 percent of the total. By suggesting that his nine content challenges "discredited" the total of *TNT*, Richard Salant was deliberately deceiving those who are unfamiliar with the problem of content analysis.

Professor Haight's comment tells you that by challenging editorial opinion, the CBS study cannot possibly rebut or refute *TNT*'s bias analysis, since that analysis rests most fundamentally on *non*-editorial opinion. The covert-editorializing aspect of *TNT* is detachable from the rest; I detach it quite clearly in Chapter V of *TNT*, called "The Parallel Principle," and in Appendix O, where I show that when all covert editorializing is removed, the bias pattern is virtually the same. By selecting the dispensable portion of *TNT* to attack and totally evading the indispensable portion, Richard Salant was compounding his deception. He was suggesting that disagreement with a microscopic portion of a *noncritical* element of *TNT* invalidated the total bias analysis.

Dr. Weinberg's comment shows that even in the area the CBS study chose to inspect, the procedure was fundamentally dishonest. By focusing in on my analysis of covert editorializing while failing to request and study my research, which contained the textual analyses of such covert opinion, the CBS study was attacking conclusions for which it had never seen the full reasoning. It was not possible for me to include a third- to a half-million words in the appendix of *TNT*, so I offered this research to readers. The "full disclosure" policy was clearly stated in *TNT*; readers have requested and received this research; scholars have studied it; it is now on file at Vanderbilt University's TV-film archives, where it can be studied along with the original videotapes. Mr. Salant, who works across the street from me, had only to ask for it before preparing his study and circulating it to the nation. He did not do so. This is why the textual analyses—closely reasoned presentations of my classifications of apparently neutral material as non-neutral—are absent from the CBS study. It is largely this absence that creates the artificial frontal lobotomy on my work, and makes it appear both irrational and arbitrary.

Professor Weinberg calls the act of publicly attacking a study without seeing its underlying data and research "indecent." The word is not too strong. At the time that Mr. Salant circulated his nationwide attack without having requested my research, I protested immediately, publicly, and angrily. I informed *Variety* that the attack was a calamitous breach of "intellectual ethics" and further described it as "malicious dishonesty" to the *St. Louis Post-Dispatch*. The entire editorial staff of *TV Guide* was distracted for days by my roars of indignation. Nothing can justify this conduct by Richard Salant. As a pioneer bias study, *TNT* has both merits and flaws; the flaws, where they exist, deserve criticism. But my work should be criticized for the thinking I actually engaged in—not for an absence of thought artificially devised by Richard Salant.

You have, finally, seen for yourself that this "indecency" and dishonesty prevails even in dealing with the material that appeared in print, *TNT* itself. Systematically, almost maniacally, Mr. Salant's team chopped out, obliterated, eliminated, misrepresented, and actively falsified my process of reasoning. The pattern is so unbroken, so consistent, that it can be laid neither to chance nor to incomprehension. A myopic idiot rolling dice would, at least once in a while, hit on *some* of the reasoning and documented evidence I supply in the book. This did not happen once.

On confronting the nature of Mr. Salant's study, a professor at the University of Massachusetts wrote to me in astonishment: "CBS is not a company—it is some kind of a Mafia!" The professor is extremely well known, the letter was private, and I will not quote his name; but I borrow his statement freely. It is rhetorical, but it captures the spirit of the situation perfectly ... with all apologies to the Mafia. Personally, I have a higher regard for an ordinary gangster than I do for educated men with the mentality of book burners.

In the last analysis that is the meaning of this CBS document: it is a kind of book burning, although mimeograph machines, not matches, were used. A book burner is a man who feels so threatened by ideas he does not understand or disagrees with, that he cannot feel safe until he has obliterated them. His choice of fire as the means of destruction is a secondary issue—the desire to obliterate is primary. That was the desire of the CBS News president—to wipe *TNT*'s ideas, to wipe its reasoning, out of existence. He used every intellectual and mechanical device available in twentieth-century America to accomplish this goal. He failed. But that he tried to destroy a book—to remove it from the marketplace—is undeniable. One expects such hostility to ideas from a John Birch primitive or from a New Left hoodlum. One should not find it in the News president of the Columbia Broadcasting Company.

One does, however—and repeatedly. In his book called *About Television*, Martin Mayer reports in detail on the dishonesties of Richard Salant in the course of the controversy over the documentary called "The Selling of the Pentagon." In this book, I report on identical types of dishonesties engaged in by the same man. Lying—the wilful obliteration of fact—is corporate policy at CBS News.

The tragedy, as Martin Mayer pointed out, is that all this lying is not necessary. It was not necessary, he says correctly, in "The Selling of the Pentagon." And I add that it was not necessary in relation to *The News Twisters*. All that was required, in the Pentagon case, was a simple concession that illegitimate editing had taken place. All that was required in the case of *The News Twisters*, was a simple concession that all men have biases, that newsmen tend to have liberal biases, that if you stuff a news department full of liberal newsmen, the department, as a whole, will probably have a liberal bias, and that the problem would be investigated. Since CBS's liberal sympathies are an open secret in the nation anyway and, since it is scarcely a crime to be a liberal, the simple truth might just as well have been told. But it was not told, in either case. Both times, senseless lies were preferred.

CONCLUSION

According to Martin Mayer, who is a kindly man, these senseless lies are told because Mr. Salant is a "lawyer" who operates on the principle of "admit nothing," even in the face of mountainous evidence to the contrary. Mr. Mayer's kindness is commendable but ill-placed. The policy of "admitting nothing" in the face of mountainous evidence—not to mention the policy of concealing, distorting, and obliterating that evidence—is not exclusively due to the habits of a "lawyer," and one cannot forgive it for that reason. Its cause lies more deeply in a corrupt belief that truth is a dispensable commodity, that public relations is a substitute for thought, and that one can fool the public indefinitely if one lays on enough stockholders' money and sets a satisfactory "father figure" in the anchorman's chair.

For one of the major news media in the United States to adopt such attitudes as top corporate policy is almost incredibly irresponsible considering the corrosive political bitterness over bias that now divides this country. Mr. Salant's policies of militant dishonesty have not just been unjust to me personally. Given the subject of the controversy, his policies are unjust and damaging to the press itself and to this country. To keep lying, idiotically, about the liberal orientation of a national news service, and increasingly enraging those to the right *and* left of that position who are fully aware that they are being lied to, is to court a disastrous reaction which can totally destroy the broadcast press and ricochet on to the print media.

Much, if not all, of the current political animosity to the networks is due not merely to bias, but to the lies themselves. Often what Mr. Salant senses as a dark "conspiracy" about him is *disgust*. These official lies simply must be stopped so that the problem can be faced and solved; and those network chieftains who believe in lying as a policy to block the solution of the problem must be exposed. That is why I have written this book.

Appendix A
Release by CBS News President Salant

Released: Oct. 11, 1971

CBS News President Richard S. Salant has made the following comments on *The News Twisters*, by Edith Efron:

"CBS News has a continuing interest in any suggestions or studies which can lead, toward more perfect achievement of the fairness and objectivity with which it presents the news. Regrettably, Miss Efron's book does not contribute to this goal.

"It purports to be a scholarly, objective analysis, supported by graphs and word counts, of the fairness with which the television networks covered seven weeks of the 1968 presidential campaign. In fact, it is nothing of the sort. It examines only a limited part of the network coverage. It does so with a distinct bias which produces gross distortions of fact. It uses statistical procedures which are seriously flawed. And it draws erroneous, prejudiced and unsupportable conclusions.

"Miss Efron's 'scientific' method is simply described. She summarizes the meaning, as she sees it, of specific broadcast stories. She decides, with nothing to guide her but her personal opinion, which of the stories are pro and which are anti the candidates and the issues selected by her for study. And she then counts the words in each category. On the basis solely of this word count, she determines whether the networks were biased for or against a candidate or an issue.

"There are many serious flaws in this approach. But there is one basic flaw which permeates and completely discredits the book.

"Its drastic conclusions, with respect to CBS News, depend entirely on the accuracy and objectivity with which Miss Efron describes and characterizes the CBS News stories on which she relies. But, in story after story, there is just no resemblance between the story as broadcast and Miss Efron's description of that story. They simply do not state what Miss Efron claims they state. She sees sinister meanings where none were intended and none exist. Her conclusions are based, in large part, on nonexistent facts.

"Since Miss Efron, generally speaking, does not quote the full, as-broadcast text of the stories mentioned in the book, it is not possible for the reader to review the accuracy of her descriptions and word counts or the validity of her pro and anti characterizations. A few of the many examples of the startling distortions which become apparent when Miss Efron's descriptions are compared with the actual broadcast text are appended."

In line with its continuing encouragement of self-analysis in order to improve its performance, and with full recognition of its responsibility to be fair and objective, CBS News has retained two highly qualified, experienced, independent research organizations, one to study the methodology used by Miss Efron and the other to review the identical 1968 campaign coverage on which her book reports. They will advise us of their conclusions when these studies have been completed, and the findings will be made public.

Appendix B
CBS Study

I

CBS News has made a spot check, for the purposes of this appendix, of the transcripts of CBS News broadcasts listed by Miss Efron in support of her conclusions. The pertinent portion of each such broadcast has been identified—and the actual broadcast text of that portion, and her pro or anti classification are quoted. These few examples, among many which can be cited, are a measure of the accuracy and fairness of her facts and conclusions.

9/25/68	*CBS News Transcript:* (Concluding paragraph in a report on Mr. Nixon's campaign visit in the Seattle area): "This week's tour, all in friendly territory, is to reassure the faithful, and to boost local GOP candidates. Nixon says he is warning his staff against over-confidence, but he himself hardly looks worried."
Appendix D (page 281)	Miss Efron classified this report as an "anti-Nixon editorial" by the reporter. Without setting out the actual words of the broadcast, Miss Efron writes that the CBS News reporter "says Nixon is over-confident; suggests he is a *liar*." (Emphasis added.)

9/16/68	*CBS News Transcript:* Humphrey: "The Rap Browns, the Stokely Carmichaels, the extremists of the left and the right will not have their way, and we will not allow them to terrorize or stampede America or cause us to lose our sense of perspective."
Appendix G (page 309)	Miss Efron classifies Mr. Humphrey's reference to extremists of the right as an "anti-conservative" attack. Her comment is: "Humphrey attacks *extremists* of the right for violence." (Emphasis added.) It is her judgment that an attack on "*extremists* of the right" is equivalent to an attack on "*conservatives.*"
9/30/68	*CBS News Transcript:* After broadcasting an excerpt from a Humphrey campaign speech, CBS News reported that Mr. Humphrey "has not, however, figured out how to handle the demonstrators. When the hecklers wish, they can dominate his campaign appearances, and that frustrates and angers Humphrey and his staff. To that extent, at least, the hecklers have the upper hand."
Appendix K (page 330)	Miss Efron classifies this report as a "pro-demonstrator editorial" by the reporter and comments: "Reporter supports demonstrators (demonstrators politically unidentified)."
10/28/68	*CBS News Transcript:* "In 1960, Richard Nixon tried to run his campaign top to bottom. This time he's found a group of smooth, intelligent, middle-class loyalists, who, like Nixon, believe in heroes, the Puritan ethic, and the American pantheon. This time he lets them work and sometimes play. The songs aboard the press plane on the electric piano soothe, they do not protest. They are more vintage Bing Crosby than Pete Seeger, and the Nixon staff is the prototype of their candidate's forgotten American. . . ."

Appendix D (page 284)	Miss Efron classifies this report as an "anti-Nixon editorial" by the reporter because "reporter describes Nixon and staff as squares who don't conform to liberal-left cultural standards; mocks their 'forgotten American' crusade."
9/25/68	*CBS News Transcript:* "From Pennsylvania, Muskie flew to Michigan and there in Taylor, a white, middle-class suburb of Detroit, was heckled by supporters of George Wallace. Correspondent Herman reports that he handled them with as much aplomb as he handled college hecklers."
Appendix H (page 312)	Miss Efron classifies this as an "anti-white middle-class editorial" by the reporter and comments: "Reporter attacks white middle class as racist."
10/28/68	*CBS News Transcript:* John Mitchell, Mr. Nixon's campaign manager describes, in a broadcast interview, the "orderly" manner in which the Republican campaign has been conducted. He concludes with this statement: "I think our operation has been, as you put it, without passion, because we have planned it and *programmed* it and have had time to carry it out." (Emphasis added.) In his wrap-up, the reporter states: "They [the Nixon staff] understand success, and in their crusade for their oppressed majority they confidently await a programmed victory."
Appendix D (page 284)	Miss Efron classifies this as an "anti-Nixon editorial" by the reporter. Failing to note that it was Mr. Nixon's campaign manager who introduced the word "programmed," she comments that the reporter compares "Nixon and staff to inhuman computers."
10/2/68	*CBS News Transcript:* "Reason itself is bruised every day. Each of the three candidates implies that as president he would drastically reduce crime,

even though crime is essentially a local problem, governors having more authority in the matter than presidents. And criminals are no respectors of political parties. The facts, which have no significance at all save to illustrate the point, are that the four states with more than 2,000 serious crimes per year per hundred thousand people, are all run by Republican governors, and in murder and manslaughter taken separately, Mr. Wallace's state of Alabama leads the nation. Humorless politics can be dangerous politics, if only because of the inevitable rude awakenings. Candidate Nixon tells us he will sweep the streets of Washington clear of prowlers and muggers. Candidate Humphrey tells us he would put an end to poverty in America. He will do in four years to eight years, in other words, what centuries of human efforts could not do. It must have been in the middle of a political campaign that a British statesman of long ago remarked 'Between craft and credulity, the voice of reason is stifled.' "

Appendix D (page 282)

Miss Efron sees in this an "anti-Nixon editorial" by the reporter because "reporter links Nixon with Wallace as law-and-order racist candidate, in contrast to over-generous humanitarian Humphrey." The meaning of this report is clear. The reporter was citing one example for each of the three major candidates to illustrate how "reason itself is bruised" by the candidates during the campaign. Miss Efron ignores the point made by the report, i.e., that Mr. Humphrey's promise to end poverty was completely unrealistic and "bruised reason." There is no basis for the charge that Mr. Nixon and Mr. Wallace are described as "racist" candidates.

10/7/68

The reporter, who is analyzing the Wallace campaign, states:

"In a real sense the Wallace movement represents a class struggle, an uprising against what he calls the pseudo-intellectuals, professors, preachers, and everything that is big—government, taxes, ownership, the big press, the big networks, the Negro movement, the left-wing student movement. All this is summed up in the word 'they.' 'It is them against us, and,' says Wallace, 'there are more of us than of them.' "

Appendix J (page 326)   Miss Efron sees in this report a "pro-left editorial" by the reporter because he "describes left-wing student movement as one of the biggest institutions in the country."

9/25/68   This report discussed an announcement by the secretary of defense that troop strength in Vietnam would not be reduced. It concluded with the following statement which is the only reference to a bombing halt:

"This interpretation of the enemy's predicament explains, at least in part, the still persisting belief that a break will come in the Paris talks. These battlefield conditions suggest that the next solid gesture toward peace may come from the enemy, but they also suggest that another solid gesture on our part may now be appropriate and fruitful, and it is on this point that the still very real argument about stopping the bombing of North Vietnam now seems to center, inside the highest councils of this government."

Appendix F (page 304)   Miss Efron classifies this as an "anti-U.S. Policy on Bombing Halt editorial." She also cites it (page 117) as a "striking" example of a report which "claims to be presenting the argument on both sides of a controversy—but in fact does not." Her conclusion (page 117) is that "the reporter is 'summing up' the argument within the administration over a bombing halt—and leaves out the arguments of Johnson-Rusk-Rostow and the generals."

Clearly, Miss Efron's assertion is unfounded. There is *no* "summing up" of the "argument within the administration." There is merely a reference to the existence of such an argument. *No* administration viewpoints, pro or con, are presented.

II

Miss Efron makes charges based on alleged but nonexistent statements in the CBS News broadcasts.

Example: Miss Efron writes (page 90):

"CBS initially relates the tale of how Muskie invited one of a group of 'leftists' to the platform. (9/25/7, Anti-Humphrey.) About nine days later CBS forgets that they were leftists. The reporter recalls that when 'stop-the-war' students heckled Muskie, he was willing to listen—but that Muskie is far less courteous to Wallace hecklers. And the CBS reporter asks Muskie why he is more impatient with 'Wallace hecklers' than with 'young, restless hecklers.' Thus the 'leftists' change into 'stop-the-war' students and then into a touching group known as 'young, restless hecklers.' (CBS, 10/4/12, Pro-'Demonstrators.')"

Miss Efron's conclusion that the 10/4/12 report constituted a pro-demonstrators editorial is based on an alleged reference, in the October 4, 1968 broadcast, to "young, *restless* hecklers." (Emphasis added.) There was no such reference. The actual reference was "young, *leftist* hecklers." Her misunderstanding of this word has led her mistakenly to charge (pages 89, 92) that CBS News editorialized by "suppressing" the political or ideological identity of hecklers and demonstrators.

Example: Miss Efron charges (Appendix I, page 317) that the reporter "attacks those who would prevent Cleaver from teaching at Berkeley as 'censors.'" But the reporter makes no reference of any kind to "censors." Miss Efron confuses "censor" with "censure" in this statement by the reporter:

"His [Cleaver's] tough talk prompted the state senate to censure the university...."

In either event, there is no basis, whatsoever, for her charge. The reporter does not "attack" the state senate for this "censure."

III

Even if one accepts Miss Efron's statistics as accurate and her methodology as sound, many of her conclusions remain unsupported by her own statistics.

Example: Miss Efron states (page 47): "on the basis of these descriptive statistics, it is clear that network coverage tends to be strongly biased in favor of the Democratic-liberal-left axis of opinion...." Yet, according to her chart (page 40), CBS broadcast 120 words *against* liberals, and *not one word for* liberals. This illustrates strikingly the invalidity of her statistical approach.

Example: Miss Efron includes an extended discussion aimed at showing that the networks favored "demonstrators" (pages 76-83). Yet her word count (page

	45) shows that CBS was against demonstrators, 1304 to 609.
Example:	Miss Efron states at the conclusion of her discussion of news coverage of George Wallace (page 61): "The coverage of opinion on George Wallace is heavily weighted against Wallace." Yet her chart (page 36) shows that CBS broadcast 1079 words for Wallace and 1282 words against him.
Example:	Miss Efron states (page 55) that the networks actively favored Hubert Humphrey and portrayed him as a "saint studded over with every virtue known to man." Yet her chart (page 33) shows that CBS broadcast 2388 words for Humphrey, only slightly more than the 2083 words against Humphrey.

IV

Miss Efron's book contains many sweeping, highly accusatory pronouncements, supported by little or no evidence or only by tortured rationalization. These extreme statements, which hardly read like scholarly conclusions by an objective analyst, provide insight into Miss Efron's own biases. This is one example:

> On ABC, reporters sanctioned violence eleven times; on CBS, nine times; and on NBC, seventeen times. In Appendix N a complete list of all references to the stories containing this opinion will be found. This quiet, steady spewing-out of justifications for violence by allegedly responsible men, under the eyes and ears of allegedly responsible network management, is a pathological phenomenon (page 95).

These are strong words. But an inspection of the transcripts of the nine CBS News broadcasts cited by Miss Efron shows no justification whatsoever for such charges. These two broadcasts are representative:

Miss Efron: Appendix E, *"Anti-Wallace, 10/22/6."* (page 296)	CBS Evening News	10/22/68

"'Hecklers' throw rocks and tomatoes at Wallace."

Kuralt: "At a rally in Oshkosh, Wisconsin, today, hecklers threw rocks, eggs and tomatoes at George Wallace. When an apple core struck him on the shoulder, Wallace dismissed it with the remark: 'That's all right, it'll wash off. That's just a bunch of anarchists.' Wallace's running mate, General Curtis LeMay, said today that integration is the answer to the nation's racial problems, and he added that he thinks George Wallace agrees with his views. At a news conference in Miami, LeMay said integration has worked in the armed forces, and it will also work in civilian life."

Miss Efron: Appendix I, *"Pro-Black Militants, 9/18/3."* (page 317)	CBS Evening News	9/18/68

"Cleaver advocates shooting of businessmen, politicians, career military, police, decision-makers."
"*Reporter sanctions Cleaver's calls for mass murder* as 'revolutionary' thought and attacks those who would prevent Cleaver from teaching at Berkeley as 'censors.'"
(Emphasis added.)

CBS News correspondent Bill Stout reports from University of California, Berkeley.

Stout: "The student protests of five years ago brought many changes to the university, including more voice for students and faculty in setting up new classes. Now sharp controversy over a course on the American social order, with the guest lecturer anti-establishment black revolutionary Eldridge Cleaver."

Cleaver: "It's the big businessmen, the politicians and these career military and police agent type people that, this is the power structure we talk about, the people who have a vested interest in the status quo, who draw their living from exploiting people through this economic system, people who live by this profit, not the people who are just plugged into the system and who have a job and go to work every day and really never manage to get their head above water. But it's the power people, the people who make the decisions in this country and who control the decision-making process in this country. Those are the enemies of the people, and those are ones who are going to be exposed and treated in a manner that they're always treated in a revolutionary situation."

Stout: " 'They ought to be shot.' Cleaver has said that again and again. When whites ask what they can do for race relations, Cleaver has said, 'Give black men machine guns.' For ten lecturers Cleaver is to get no state salary, but will be paid from student funds. His tough talk prompted the state senate to censure the university, and brought criticism from two men who otherwise rarely agree."

Governor Ronald Reagan: "I'm opposed from the simple standpoint that I think it is ridiculous to bring someone on as a supposed instructor or lecturer, which is the way he was to be brought on, who has absolutely no qualifications whatsoever for that position."

> Jesse Unruh: "I think clearly it's very, very difficult to defend the appointment of Mr. Cleaver as a lecturer. I think that it's an unfortunate choice and represents almost a death wish on the part of those people participating in it insofar as the university is concerned."
>
> Stout: "Cleaver is thirty-three. He's done time on narcotics and assault convictions and was in court this week on fresh charges of assault and attempted murder. He faces trial for that later in the year. But the university regents meet tomorrow to consider demands they overrule the selection of Cleaver as guest lecturer. Bill Stout, CBS News, Los Angeles."
>
> By no stretch of the imagination did the reporter "sanction Cleaver's calls for mass murder." Nor does the transcript support Miss Efron's charge that the reporter "attacked" any persons as "censors." In any event, the word actually used was "censures" not "censors."

This is another example of a sweeping, highly accusatory but unfounded charge. Miss Efron states (page 61) that network coverage of the George Wallace campaign "editorially sanctions the physical attacks upon him." In support of this serious accusation, she states (page 58) that "language customarily used to describe those who engage in physical assault." This, she concludes, was "a tacit sanctioning of the assaultive conduct." And, finally, on page 59, she lists a total of three CBS News broadcasts which describe, as "hecklers" and "dissenters," people who throw "rocks," "an egg," and "objects" at Mr. Wallace.

CBS Comment: The word used by CBS News was "dissidents" and not "dissenters," as Miss Efron states. In any event, it is hardly realistic or accurate to conclude that use of the terms "hecklers" and "dissidents" constituted an *"editorial sanction"* of physical attacks upon Mr. Wallace—particularly since each of the broadcasts explicitly reported the physical acts involved.

V

These are two additional examples which illustrate how Miss Efron's statements can mislead:

Example: Miss Efron states (page 32) that, during the study period of seven weeks on which her conclusions are based, there were only 320 "words spoken for" Mr. Nixon on the CBS Evening News. A quick check of the broadcast transcripts shows that, during the period in question, the CBS Evening News carried a total of 4747 words spoken *only by Mr. Nixon* in the course of his campaign—and presumably spoken in his own behalf as a candidate. But this fact does not appear in the book. Certainly, it is pertinent to an evaluation of the coverage given to Mr. Nixon.

Example: Miss Efron states (page 76) that "CBS viewers are not informed of undercover testimony against the Yippies." She is referring to testimony before a congressional committee about Yippie plans "to bomb buildings, kill policemen and assassinate candidates." The October 3, 1968 broadcast of the CBS Evening News included the following:

Cronkite: " 'A witness told a congressional hearing today that Yippie leader Jerry Rubin talked of killing presidential candidates and overthrowing the government during the disorders accompanying the Democratic convention. Rubin was in the hearing room to testify later, and he shouted out a protest about "this worm's lies" as Illinois undercover agent Robert Pierson testified. One leftist witness walked out of the hearing, another refused to testify about any Communist affiliation, and a third was arrested as he arrived wearing a shirt which appeared to have been made from an American flag. While the hearing continued, other Yippies milled around outside until police moved in.' "

Appendix C
"Analysis of Method"

A document circulated by CBS on October 11, 1971, along with the CBS study.

Summary and Critique (by Edith Efron)

The document which follows is not an analysis of "method." It is a collection of seven random arguments—six dependent upon evasion, one irrelevant to *TNT*. Here are the major points and my answers to them:

- CBS takes exception to the very concept of a limited pro-and-con opinion study on controversial subjects in the news. (CBS is evading the fact that a controversy *is* a clash of opinion—and that if one is to examine the coverage of controversy, it is the pro and con opinion one must examine. CBS is tacitly objecting to *any* inspection of its news coverage of controversies.)
- CBS complains that seven weeks, the critical two-thirds of the campaign period, is insufficient time in which to ascertain such fairness. (CBS is evading the fact that if its coverage of campaign-related controversies has

not been fair by Election day, it has not been fair: time has run out.)

• CBS argues that it is very difficult to determine objectively and accurately whether an opinion is "for" or "against," e.g., "for" or "against" a candidate or the war. (CBS is evading the fact that its individual reporters make such identifications routinely—i.e., "endorses," "opposes," "heckles," "supports," "dissents," "praises," "anti-war demonstration," "a rally for x," "cheering," "booing," etc.—and that CBS stoutly defends their objectivity and accuracy.)

• CBS charges *TNT* with ignoring the exigencies of "spot news." (CBS is evading the fact that *TNT* accepts network event selection as a given of the study; it is only the selection of opinion *within* the coverage of events that *TNT* challenges.)

• CBS charges *TNT* with evaluation of the "impact" on a viewer in terms of the "length" of a statement. (CBS evades the fact that *TNT* nowhere discusses the "impact" of any given opinion on viewers at all; *TNT*'s only sources of information about viewer attitudes are the Gallup and Harris polls, indicating that viewers' conclusions about 1968 bias conform generally with *TNT*'s finding on broad bias patterns.)

• CBS charges me with having said, in 1964, that I saw no way to solve the bias problem. (CBS is evading that human phenomenon called "learning": it is clearly stated in *TNT* that I worked for one year to solve the problem, and that *TNT* itself is the solution I offer.)

• CBS offers *five* different "theoretical" reasons for which a network might carry far fewer words from one presidential candidate than from another. (This issue is irrelevant to *TNT*; *TNT* quotes candidates, like anyone else, on the issues examined by the study, and does not compare total Nixon speech on all subjects to total Humphrey speech on all subjects. CBS is actually having a private anxiety attack over the Equal Time Law, camouflaged as an argument with *TNT*.)

APPENDIX 155

This "Analysis of Method" had no particular impact on *TNT*, save to confuse those who had not read the book. Here is the original CBS document:

Analysis of Method Used by Miss Efron

1) Miss Efron's method:
She selected a list of what she considered the pertinent issues of the 1968 campaign, including—of course—the candidates.

She decided that a limited seven-week look (Monday through Friday), at only one television broadcast series (the Evening News), on each of the three networks, would enable her to determine (i) the fairness with which the networks covered her selected issues, and (ii) in general, the fairness with which the networks cover all controversial issues.

She decided that it was *completely* unnecessary, for this purpose, to consider what was included, during the seven-week period, on any of the many other broadcasts carried by the networks.[1]

She decided that only those words which expressed *partisan* opinions about her selected issues were pertinent. Yet she chose to ignore the words spoken by the candidates themselves. Mr. Nixon, for example, spoke a total of 4,747 words, in various stories carried on the CBS Evening News (Monday through Friday) in the seven weeks under examination. Clearly such coverage was most effective, from his viewpoint, and, certainly, it was partisan.

She decided that the extent to which the networks carried neutral nonpartisan words was *completely* irrelevant to a determination of the fairness and nonpartisanship with which they covered her selected issues.

She decided, by examining the transcripts of the broadcasts (or summaries of the transcripts), which words constituted partisan opinions about her selected issues.

She decided which of those words were pro and which were anti and totaled the words in each category. It is those word counts that are the basis for her serious charges.

2) The various decisions, by their nature, required innumerable

subjective judgments—presumably by Miss Efron. If her method was to have any semblance of accuracy, it was essential that these judgments be completely objective and completely insulated from her personal opinions. But this is an assignment which Miss Efron, herself, considers "impossible." At least she did in 1964:

> [I]t is *impossible* for a human being to combine words or pictures without smuggling in value judgments. [Emphasis added.] (*TV Guide*, April 11, 1964)

In the same article she writes:

> ... Congressman Oren Harris (D., Ark.) commented further: "We get into the problem of deciding whether a news analysis is editorializing when it is slanted.... *Who is going to decide? Isn't it largely how we might feel as individuals toward a particular news report?*" With this question, Mr. Harris isolates the central and unresolved dilemma of the Fairness Doctrine. *In any given news report or documentary on a controversial issue, a treatment that seems eminently "fair," "impartial" or "objective" to one viewer, may seem eminently "unfair," "slanted" and "biased" to another.* The truth is that the Fairness Doctrine contains a set of noble abstractions to which most would subscribe in principle—but upon which *no two appear to agree in practical application.* [Emphasis added.]

And a recent FCC release (Report No. 10089; August 20, 1971), on a different but related subject, reports "the Commission said ... it is a 'wholly impracticable quagmire for this agency to attempt to evaluate' how much 'partisan' material is contained in a particular report" (by the President or other public officials).

3) How then did Miss Efron perform this "impossible" assignment which is so basic to the accuracy of her method? Did she find it possible, with complete objectivity and free from the influence of her personal opinions, to separate the partisan from the nonpartisan, the factual from the slanted, and the pro from

the anti? The answer is emphatically negative. Some of the many examples are included in the appendix to the statement by Richard S. Salant issued for release on October 11, 1971.

Specific Defects of Her Method

1) The use of word counts as a measure of fairness may be invalid and misleading even if the word counts are accurate and objective. These are some of the reasons:

> a) It assumes, incorrectly, that the impact of a statement is measured solely by its length. Surely, the source of the statement (e.g., a universally respected nonpartisan as contrasted with a prejudiced political supporter), the manner of delivery, the substance of what is said, and the subtleties of of emotion and emphasis are all factors which must be considered in evaluating the impact. But Miss Efron gives no weight to any of these factors—which, inevitably, makes for distorted results. A forceful speaker, for example, can say in ten words what a rambling speaker needs one hundred words to say. And the ten words may well have greater impact. But, in those circumstances, the Efron method would nevertheless record a ten to one bias against the forceful speaker.
>
> b) It ignores the basic journalistic consideration which determines, of necessity, what spot news will be included in a hard news broadcast. The determining factor, on any particular day, must be newsworthiness— and not an arbitrary decision to balance opinions.[2] Coverage of a riot on the streets of Detroit, for example, should not be shelved in favor of a quiet interview with Roy Wilkins in his home merely because an interview with Cleaver was carried in a prior broadcast. We must cover the news as it breaks. Consequently, the total spot news coverage in the Evening News during the course of any campaign will be the total of what was news-

worthy on each individual day of that campaign. And, if this produces an imbalance in words, it is obviously erroneous to conclude, as Miss Efron does, that the imbalance *must* be attributable to bias. The soundness of the news judgments made on each day is a factor that must be assessed in the light of everything that happened on that day. Miss Efron has neither the information nor, apparently, the inclination, to make this assessment.

c) The volume of newsworthy words generated by a political campaign depends, in large part, on the specific campaign tactics and strategy of the candidates. For example:

i) If one candidate campaigns more frequently and more vigorously than the other candidate, he is likely to generate more news. Mr. Humphrey, in 1968, campaigned strenuously and continuously. But Mr. Nixon, as a matter of strategy, for at least part of the time, deliberately conducted a low-key, low-profile campaign. For example, at one point in the campaign (in early October), Mr. Nixon took a five-day hiatus for strategy meetings in Key Biscayne, Florida, and later in the month (October 20 and 21), he held similar meetings in New York City.

ii) One candidate may stress public appearances. Another candidate may stress the use of paid political broadcasts with a format he considers advantageous such as, for example, the paid political broadcasts around the country where Mr. Nixon, in a studio, answered questions put to him by panels selected by the local Republicans.

iii) The out party tends to concentrate a good deal of its fire on the deficiencies of the incumbent and his administration rather than on the new candidate. Consequently, for a proper perspective, the words in the Evening News which attacked LBJ and the Democratic administration should be added to the "anti-Humphrey words." Miss Efron does not seem to have done this. It should be noted that for at least part of the

1968 campaign, Mr. Nixon muted his attacks on Mr. Humphrey personally, whereas Mr. Humphrey attacked vigorously during the entire campaign.

iv) A word count limited to words of "opinion" which is what Miss Efron claims for her word count, is not an accurate reflection of political coverage because it does not accurately reflect the coverage given to the candidate who takes the "high road." If, for example, a candidate who talks about Vietnam is given one minute, and a candidate who rises in praise of God, mother and apple pie is given four minutes, the former will be included in the Efron count. The latter will not, despite the fact that he had more exposure. This, too, makes for distorted results. The candidate who concentrates on opinions will show up more frequently in the Efron word counts than the candidate who concentrates on generalities.

v) If, on a particular day, one candidate makes a new proposal, or a new criticism, or states a point with special forcefulness, it is more likely to be used than a tired, frequently repeated speech made on that day by the other candidate.

d) Miss Efron ignores the logistics involved in putting together a news broadcast. Since there are deadlines which must be met, it is inevitable that some speeches, and some paid political broadcasts, and some events, will occur too late for inclusion in the Evening News. It is essential, therefore, in determining whether bias exists, to compare the Evening News choice of stories on any day with the stories actually available to it for use on that day. Newsworthy stories which come in too late for inclusion in the Evening News will sometimes be included in other broadcasts. But, for whatever the reason, in formulating her conclusions, Miss Efron failed to look at those other broadcasts.

A word count which fails to take these various factors into account is obviously incomplete, inadequate, and meaningless. Miss Efron took none of them into account.

2) As one small example of the inequity of the limited Efron look at the broadcast schedule, she discusses for pages her thesis that the networks, including CBS, *completely* ignored the rank-and-file blacks, their achievements and viewpoints. She makes no mention of, and gives no weight to, the CBS News series, "Of Black America"—in particular "Portrait in Black and White"—which did exactly what she says was not done. While it is true that this series of seven broadcasts ended on September 2, 1968 and, therefore, did not fall within the seven-week period at which she was looking, it immediately preceded that period and her failure even to mention it adds sizably to the distorted picture she is painting.

Miss Efron either is not aware of—or chooses to ignore—the time limitations placed upon a network television news broadcast, particularly during a presidential campaign. It is unlikely that a hard news broadcast will be able to deal comprehensively with philosophic or "non-event" issues which are not in the mainstream of the campaign. In fact, many of these issues lend themselves not to hard news coverage at all, but to documentary coverage. Most of the issues Miss Efron criticizes were in fact covered in documentary form—among them, the aforementioned "Of Black America"; "The New Left"; "Generations Apart"—a three-part series; numerous Vietnam specials; "The College Turmoil"; "Black Power—White Backlash"; and "Viet Cong";—before, during and after 1968. Miss Efron's oversight only serves to emphasize the inadequacy and inequity of using one seven-week period and one broadcast series as the sole basis for an indictment as serious as the one made by her.

3) There are, obviously, many stories which do not lend themselves to pro or anti categorization. For example, Miss Efron has an entry for October 15, 1968, in which she states (page 296) that "Hippies heckle Wallace by cheering him." This refers to a report in which the correspondent describes how Mr. Wallace was heckled by members of a crowd chanting, "We want Wallace." The correspondent went on to say: "It was bound to happen. The hippies, those whom George Wallace calls anarchists, decided to come to one of his rallies and put on a different kind of show." Miss Efron classifies this report as "anti-Wallace." Clearly, this is a subjective evaluation, which makes it obvious that there is no coldly scien-

tific approach to the categorization process, as Miss Efron professes. It is fair to assume that if a large number of viewers concluded that this report was "anti-Wallace," as many—or more—would construe a report that Mr. Wallace had been "heckled" by "hippies," to be in fact "pro-Wallace."

4) Miss Efron's failure to add a "neutral" (factual) category to her pro and anti categories creates the distorted and unrealistic impression of network coverage that is totally opinionated. It also leaves her study hanging in mid-air. If it was, in fact, her intention to determine whether network coverage was partisan or nonpartisan, how could she possibly ignore the extent to which the network words were nonpartisan?

5) Miss Efron has counted, as "opinion," material which represents straightforward factual reporting of statements or events. And, as already indicated, her tendency has been to color these factual reports with her own personal prejudices. If a candidate is having difficulties raising funds, or is showing the physical strain of the campaign, or is having his rallies or speeches disrupted by demonstrators, the correspondent who reports this is reporting something that is true. He is following one of the basic tenets of professional journalism—the criterion of accuracy—a criterion that Miss Efron does not acknowledge nor make provision for in her study.

Appendix D
Winick Study (as summarized by Broadcasting)

Doubts About Data in Efron Book

Arbitrary Categorizing in Analyzing News Programs, Oversight of Other Factors Cited in Rebuttal for CBS News

An independent study commissioned by CBS News questions sharply the methodology employed by Edith Efron in examining the content of network television news programs, described in her book, *The News Twisters* (*Broadcasting*, September 27 et seq.).

The critique, released last week, was made by Dr. Charles Winick, professor of sociology at the City University of New York, who has conducted content analyses of TV programs, fan mail, motion pictures and other outlets of communications.

A second study commissioned by CBS News which is to be completed shortly, will review CBS News's coverage of the final seven weeks of the 1968 presidential campaign on "CBS Evening News with Walter Cronkite," the period cited in Miss Efron's book, which ascribes a "Democratic-liberal-radical-left axis of opinion" to network news. It is being conducted by International Research Associates Inc., New York.

Dr. Winick's central complaint was that Miss Efron's book in its analysis of news programs does not recognize some of the accepted practices in the field.

For example, *The News Twisters* concerns itself only with the 7 p.m. network news during the pre-election period, Dr. Winick noted. He claimed this is not representative of the total news programming of the day, or of news broadcasts at other times of the year.

"A sample of broadcast news chosen for content analysis should be reasonably representative of all broadcast news," he asserted. "By selecting a pre-election period, *The News Twisters* is essentially presenting a study of pre-election coverage."

Dr. Winick suggested that "a much fairer procedure" would have been to sample news broadcasts at other times of the year when there would be "a greater spectrum of both content and opinion" than is possible before election.

He also observed that a study of network coverage of news should embrace more than one program, which may be subject to special considerations in terms of content because of its brevity, time of broadcast, differences among time zones and responsiveness to "hard news."

But even with respect to the 7 p.m. network news, Dr. Winick pointed out, less than one-fourth of the total number of words broadcast was coded, and neutral or nonpartisan material was not considered. He felt that the latter material might be classified as "neutral" or could be placed in a "balanced" category to provide a fuller and more valid content analysis.

Dr. Winick claimed that key-coding categories and concepts are not clearly defined in the book and neither intensity nor degree of opinion was systematically measured. He said the word count of "pro" and "anti" opinion, the basic quantitative procedure used in the book, is "probably less desirable than other measures might have been."

A "word count restricted to opinions may not accurately measure the content of a story in terms of how it will be perceived by the viewer," he said. "A long story which implicitly conveys the overall thrust of being on one side of an issue but expresses no explicit opinion for that side might contain a one sentence opinion which would be tabulated on the other side."

He criticized *The News Twisters* for not considering the impact of the communicator, quoting Miss Efron as saying, "It does not matter who is voicing the opinions—it matters only what opinions are being voiced." "If George Ball says, 'Humphrey should get the Negro vote,' it would be clearly pro-Humphrey; the same remark from George Wallace would have to be classified as anti-Humphrey."

Another shortcoming of Miss Efron's methodology, according to Dr. Winick, is its reliance on only the sound aspect of network television news and the absence of consideration of the impact of the visual content. He contended that the voice, phrasing, gestures, and timing of a communicator can "substantially contribute to the direction and intensity of what he is saying."

Dr. Winick stressed that in content analysis the issue of reliability is important, particularly in studies of controversial material where a coder's bias may intrude in spite of himself. He said the "non-use of any reliability procedures" in *The News Twisters* is, "in the view of the seriousness of its charges, a barrier to its credibility."

Appendix E
UPI Reporter (Tatarian story)

Office of Roger Tatarian
Vice-President and Editor

United Press International
220 East 42nd Street
New York, N.Y. 10017

October 28, 1971

    One of the joys of flying long distances is that you finally get around to the book that has so long been demanding to be read. If there is an occasional inflight distraction, it is a pleasant one: Steak or chicken Kiev? White wine or red? More pleasant distractions, certainly, than the insistent ring of the telephone or the imperious, five-bell summons from the tele-printer bespeaking crisis or calamity. All of that is now 39,000 feet and thousands of miles away.

    But it is precisely this isolation that proves frustrating when the book you are reading is Edith Efron's *The News Twisters* (Nash, $7.95). For on almost every page there is an assertion so damning to network news broadcasts that no trained newsman could possibly accept them without an independent check.

    So the best you can do while traveling is to promise yourself that nothing will get a higher priority on your return home than a personal examination of the basis on which Miss Efron presents her charges of rampant political, racial and cultural bias in the news programs of the three major networks. Although her target is network news, her book will doubtless give encouragement to those who regard all news media with suspicion and mistrust. It is thus of equal interest to all of us.

Miss Efron has been on the staff of *TV Guide* for about ten years. She is not necessarily accountable for the summary of her book that appears on the dust jacket; that overheated prose is presumably the work of her publisher's publicity department. Still, even discounting its tone, it does serve as a fair precis of what is inside. Here are two sample paragraphs:

"*The News Twisters*, as its distinguished readers say on the back cover of this book, is a 'bombshell' and a 'blockbuster.' Its initials—*TNT*—are not a coincidence. A powerfully documented exposé of bias in network news, it explodes the myth of network fairness and reduces the networks' claim of political neutrality to rubble. . . .

"*TNT* slashes through the conventional political line-ups on the network bias issue—uniting all of them in one scholarly yet suspenseful analysis. It confirms Republican charges of a calculated assault on Richard Nixon. It confirms the multiparty 'Silent Majority' charges of left-liberal bias. It confirms black-minority charges of insidious racism. And it confirms New Left charges of distortion and 'censorship.' "

Those are grave charges, and Miss Efron thus makes her work one that simply cannot be overlooked by anyone interested in responsible journalism. So you begin to look carefully at her evidence.

Her study was based on the prime time news broadcasts of ABC, CBS and NBC during seven weeks of the 1968 presidential campaign. These were generally the news programs aired between 7:00 and 7:30 p.m. Miss Efron picked them because "they are known to be the major source of political information for the whole country."

Miss Efron had all of these broadcasts recorded and then analyzed them to determine which positions they took on the candidates and on major issues of the day like the Vietnam war and campus violence.

The early part of the book is devoted to a series of graphs showing the number of words for and against the candidates. On

ABC, she found 869 words for Nixon and 7493 against; on CBS, 320 for Nixon and 5300 against; and on NBC, 431 for and 4234 against.

When it came to Hubert Humphrey, Miss Efron's count showed: ABC, 4218 for, 3569 against; CBS, 2388 for, 2083 against; and NBC, 1852 for and 2655 against.

The nagging question that arises very early is precisely how Miss Efron defines a word "for" or "against" a candidate and whether she uses standards that would be generally accepted. Alas, you cannot answer that at 39,000 feet; Miss Efron does not present the actual texts on which she bases her analyses and this, in fact, is the fatal flaw in her case.

This omission strikes you repeatedly as you read Miss Efron's evaluation of various items from the three networks.

For example, on page 281, she writes that on September 25, 1968, a CBS reporter "says Nixon has a rancorous streak; says Nixon is overconfident; suggests he is a liar."

If this is what the CBS reporter said, Miss Efron's charge of bias is proved. But when you get the actual text from CBS, you find that what the reporter said was: "This week's tour, all in friendly territory, is to reassure the faithful, and to boost local GOP candidates. Nixon says he is warning his staff against over-confidence, but he himself hardly looks worried."

Again, on page 312, Miss Efron lists a CBS broadcast of September 25, 1968, in which, in her words, "Reporter attacks white middle class as racists." According to CBS, the precise words which Miss Efron interpreted in this manner were: "From Pennsylvania, Muskie flew to Michigan and there in Taylor, a white, middle-class suburb of Detroit, was heckled by supporters of George Wallace. Correspondent Herman reports he handled them with as much aplomb as he handled college hecklers."

On page 285, she portrays an NBC broadcast of September 20, 1968, in these words: "Reporter suppresses intensity of Nixon's triumph in Democratic Philadelphia as reported by two other networks, and devotes whole story to 'proving' that it was not a success at all, that the crowds were not for Nixon."

When you get the full text from NBC, this is what you find:

> Chet Huntley is off tonight. I'm David Brinkley, NBC News.

> When a candidate campaigns downtown in a big city ... it is wise to arrive during the lunch hour ... to catch the maximum number of people on the streets ... whether they came out to see him or not.
>
> Vice-President Humphrey rode through Philadelphia at mid-day two weeks ago ... and Richard Nixon was there at mid-day today.
>
> The city generally is Democratic ... but those who saw both candidates there say—for whatever it may prove—that Nixon's crowd was bigger.
>
> In any case ... Nixon's turnout was large ... and here's a report from NBC News Correspondent Herbert Kaplow.
>
> **Kaplow:** Nixon came here knowing that his opponent didn't get much of a reception here a week or so—Nixon was determined to do better, and apparently has—So, this is more fuel for Nixon's fast start.
>
> His campaign is diverse, as we saw during this past week. Not only did he move into an urban center such as Philadelphia—there were visits to smaller, and different type communities—Salt Lake City; Fresno, California; Springfield, Missouri; and Peoria, Illinois.
>
> It was the kind of political situation Nixon likes—technically, he was in the enemy camp—but it was a weak enemy—and so he rode through downtown Philadelphia looking more like the hero, than the man who technically should've been the hero, Hubert Humphrey.

Far too often, when Miss Efron's characterization of a broadcast is weighed against the text, it is revealed to reflect only her own very subjective evaluation of a series of words that can and do convey something quite different to others.

The great pity about Miss Efron's book is that it is going to be seized upon and cited by critics of the media in general as proof of everything they have always said about the press. They, like Miss Efron herself, forget that communication is a two-way process, and that it is not always the sender who twists facts; the receiver can do it quite as easily. Miss Efron proves that she herself excels at it.

ROGER TATUM

Appendix F
Testimony of Edith Efron before the Senate Subcommittee on Constitutional Rights, February 2, 1972

Senator Ervin, Members of the Committee:

A view has crystallized in this country that the bias controversy is a relatively new phenomenon, spawned by a repressive Nixon administration, and bred in the dark shadows of right-wing conspiracies.

This view is a symptom of our anti-historical age, where memories are increasingly confined to the parameters of the daily press.

The bias controversy was actually born in the thirties with the collectivist concept of public ownership of the airwaves. Until that time, if people did not like the bias of a publication or a news service, they solved the problem by refusing, individually, to buy it—a simple and rational system that still prevails in all media save broadcast news. It is when the people were informed by the United States Government that they collectively "owned" the airwaves, and were quasi-proprietors of the broadcast press, that they began to haggle collectively over the political orientation of that press.

The government took its first drastic action to control bias in 1941, when the FCC, with its Mayflower Decision, deprived all American broadcasters of their First Amendment rights by forbidding them to express their own views on controversial issues. This solved the bias problem satisfactorily: there were no longer any controversial views on the air to get excited about. Unfortunately, the solution was more deadly than the problem: it constituted a frontal lobotomy of the entire broadcast medium. America had to endure eight years of government-induced vacancy in a major communications system—and the marks of the lobotomy have never disappeared—before the error was acknowledged and corrected.

The correction did not take the form of restoring unbreached First Amendment rights to the individual broadcaster; he remained a second-class citizen. It took the form, in 1949, of the Fairness Doctrine—which allowed the broadcaster to express his own opinions on major controversies, provided that he gave "equal," "equally forceful" and "nonpartisan" coverage to other points of view as well.

And from 1949 to this present day, there has been constant dissension in this country over the problem of fairness in broadcast news. It has been most acute with respect to network news which, by virtue of government permission and protection, has acquired a monopoly over the nationwide dissemination of the facts and interpretations of American political life.

As a staff writer on *TV Guide*, I have been covering this constantly simmering antagonism to the political attitudes in network news for ten years. It was a serious problem in 1960. By 1964, under the Kennedy administration, the anger had become so intense that it inspired a congressional investigation. And by 1968, under the Johnson administration, this anger exploded like a bombshell—with nationwide protests being registered over network coverage of the race riots, the Republican convention, the Democratic convention, the anti-war riots in Chicago. The number of Americans by then who felt that network news was biased ranged between 57 and 70 percent, according to polls of the period.

Throughout this remarkable decade of mounting protest, network management has militantly refused to grant that there is the slightest basis in reality for these public reactions. It has attributed them to a variety of neurotic responses ranging from selective perception, through escapist intolerance of bad news, to a hostile desire to kill the messenger who brought the bad news. Apart from this parlor psychoanalysis of the majority of the population, the networks have had nothing to say save to attest with regularity to their own impeccably objective perceptions.

It was in 1968, at the height of the nationwide protests against network bias that I undertook to do a study of my own—a study of how the networks covered the critical two-thirds of the presidential campaign of 1968, the last seven weeks until Election Day. I was given a small grant to cover taping, typing and research expenses by the New York Historical Research Foundation, and I set to work.

Time does not permit an extensive presentation of my theory and method, but I will mention three points:

First, I concentrated on prime-time news alone, because all studies indicate that these early-evening news programs are the most important source of political information for the majority of the country.

Second, I used an intrinsically journalistic observation as my key test for bias. There is one slanting device known to every editor and reporter in the land. It is this: if a reporter wishes to load coverage of a controversy in favor of a certain position—he will simply stuff his coverage with opinions from those who take the desired position, while giving little or no room to opinions from the other side. There are other far more subtle editorial slanting techniques—in *The News Twisters*, I name and illustrate thirty-three of them—but this is the central one on which my entire analysis is based: I did a systematic check on the equity of pro and con opinion on a group of controversial subjects. This test simultaneously served to check on the network's adherence to the Fairness Doctrine.

Third and last: I selected the major controversial subjects of the period: The presidential race, the war, black militancy, left-wing protest movements, and several sub-aspects of these broad subjects. In classifying opinion on these matters as pro and con, my basic rule was always to conform to the reports' own classifications where they existed. If, for example, a reporter described an opinion as "heckling" or "opposition" or as "booing," I classified it as antagonistic opinion; if he described it as "endorsement" or "support" or as "cheering," I classified it as favorable or pro-opinion. The great bulk of opinion in the study turned out to be of this variety which already came pre-categorized in one way or another by the reporter. The opinion which I classified independently was usually covert or implicit opinion by reporters.

That, in essence, was my method. I applied it systematically to seven weeks of network coverage—300,000 words. And the results appeared in *The News Twisters*. I will not report on all my findings here. Instead, I will give you a close-up view of the results of my investigations into two of the most important controversies of the 1968 period—the Nixon-Humphrey race and the war.

The results on Mr. Nixon alone have caused the greatest consternation. Speaking quantitatively, in terms of simple word count, the pro and con opinion on the Republican candidate for the presidency ran as follows:

> 16 to 1 against Nixon on CBS
> 10 to 1 against Nixon on NBC
> 8.5 to 1 against Nixon on ABC

The anti-Nixon opinion is so voluminous in contrast to the pro-Nixon opinion that it verges on the ludicrous. The content of most of this criticism itself cannot be challenged. Most of the attacks on Nixon were journalistically legitimate. They came from Democratic party and Independent party challengers, from assorted Democratic party politicians, from Democratic union chiefs, and, as such, were a valid part of the campaign.

What was bizarre was primarily the quantity and repetitiousness of the criticism, often in purely optional matters. To illustrate: on CBS, Nixon was charged with telling untruths seven times by political opponents—twice by Hubert Humphrey, twice by Wallace, once by Ramsey Clark, once by Clark Clifford, and once by Lawrence O'Brien. But NBC and ABC deemed such charges newsworthy only three times each. Thus, CBS viewers heard politicians charge Nixon with dishonesty more often than did the viewers on the other two networks put together. All one can conclude is that CBS particularly liked to air this charge.

Similarly, the degree of hostile editorialization about Nixon, his personality, his morality, his campaign techniques, and so on, was quite voluminous. ABC viewers were privileged to hear Nixon described as a man who went for his enemies' "jugular" and who would like to assault them with a "meat-axe."

Startling as was the vast body of anti-Nixon opinion, even more startling were the pro-Nixon findings. In their way, these are the most deadly.

Here, for example, is a summary of all pro-Nixon opinion, from the public and from Republican political figures, carried by CBS-TV News during the seven weeks of the campaign period studied:

- On only *six* days during the entire seven-week period did CBS News's stories include opinion favorable to Nixon from members of the public.

- On only *one* day during the seven-week period—on October 28, towards the very end of the campaign—did CBS News's stories include any Republican political opinion which praised Richard Nixon. It came specifically, from Dwight and Mamie Eisenhower, and from Nixon assistants Patrick Buchanan and Raymond Price.

The picture is even bleaker for Nixon on ABC-TV. ABC news stories also reported only six times in seven weeks on opinions favoring Nixon from the public. And as for Republican political figures: once, on October 8, ABC News informed its viewers that Senator Javits supported Nixon. Unless one wants to count Bud Wilkinson as a Republican political figure—there was no more.

Of the three networks, NBC was most generous. NBC viewers actually heard opinions favorable to Nixon from the public twelve times in seven weeks. And NBC cited four Republican politicians, on four different days as having favorable attitudes to Nixon. They were: Senator Dirksen, Representative Gerald Ford, Vice-Presidential candidate Spiro Agnew, and State Senator David Stanley.

Given facts like these, one need hardly look at the anti-Nixon opinion at all to know that this was politically biased coverage. The opinions of American citizens who supported Nixon, and the opinions of the Republican Party representatives who were working to elect him president, were simply not on the air.

By contrast, the coverage of Humphrey was fair. Most network newsmen were not enamored of Humphrey—at least not until he had come out for a unilateral bombing halt and won the support of the anti-war groups; but by the end of the campaign period, pro- and anti-Humphrey opinion was fairly equitable on all three networks—with ABC and CBS being a touch more friendly, and NBC a touch less. In general, the early sources of political antagonism to Humphrey were thoroughly explored by the reporters; and the later sources of support were given a full airing.

My statistical findings on the presidential race have aroused something of an uproar in the country. And inevitably, a great many people are frantically denying their reality and are charging me with writing fiction, most particularly in the area of the Nixon findings. You will be interested, therefore, in the comments made in the Winter issue of *The Public Interest* by Professor Paul H. Weaver of the Harvard University Department of Government. He writes as follows:

> ... [T]here are three points to be made about this problem. First, my own inspection of two different samples of Miss Efron's file of anti-Nixon opinion convinces me that, by any reasonable standard, the large majority of such items are in fact quite clearly anti-Nixon opinion; no more than 20 or 30 percent of the anti-Nixon items might be questioned. Nobody has shown that the proportion of questionable items is larger; indeed, so far critics have merely adduced a few extreme examples, as if these were enough to invalidate the entire study. And this brings me to the second point. What is significant about Miss Efron's findings is not the absolute numbers of words pro and con; it is the *relative size* of the two bodies of opinion. In order to invalidate the finding of a huge disparity between pro-Nixon and anti-Nixon opinion, it is not enough to show that *some* anti-Nixon opinion has been incorrectly classified—one must show that *most* of it has been

incorrectly classified. Even if one were to find that she had overestimated the amount of anti-Nixon opinion by 100 percent and underestimated the amount of pro-Nixon opinion by 50 percent, there would still be 2.5 times more anti-Nixon opinion than pro-Nixon opinion, a clearly "unfair" pattern. Needless to say, nobody has yet established errors of this magnitude, and it seems unlikely that anyone will.

You will also be interested in a statement issued to the press on October 27 of last year by Dr. George Weinberg. Dr. Weinberg is a psychologist, a research consultant, a statistician, and author of one of the leading statistics texts in use in American colleges and universities for the past decade. Dr. Weinberg said:

> I saw Miss Efron's research before reading her book and before knowing her conclusions. I found that my judgments coincided with hers well over 90 percent of the time. The great majority of the statements she classifies as pro or con opinion could hardly be classified otherwise. Miss Efron is far more objective, systematic and explicit in her method than anyone known to me who has ever written a book about TV. After examining her data, I believe that any systematic tabulation by any method would result in essentially the same findings.

In brief, I have not been writing fiction.

Given these findings on Nixon the question inevitably comes up: Was this bias deliberate? The answer to this question is complex and I cannot do justice to it in a few words. But briefly my own answer is this: it was not deliberate in the sense of an organized plot or of a conscious cabal. But it was inevitable given the virtually all-liberal composition of network staffs.

During the campaign, Eric Sevareid acknowledged on the air that most newsmen were for Hubert Humphrey—leaving to implication the fact that most were against Richard Nixon. On February 8, 1970 Howard K. Smith brought this implication out into the open. He generally confirmed Vice-President Agnew's charges and said this about the newsmen's prejudices: "Johnson was politically assassinated and some are trying to assassinate Nixon politically. They hate Richard Nixon irrationally."

I believe that my findings are evidence of such antagonism, that it was so deep and widespread that it contaminated professional decisions—and that network managements must be held responsible for the result.

Now, to examine another subject, briefly—the war.

In *The News Twisters*, opinion on the Vietnam war is classified under different headings, just as it appeared in network news stories. There is: opinion on the U.S. war policy in general; and opinion on the U.S. bombing halt policy in particular.

And once again, we see precisely the same pattern of heavy loading of opinion on one side—and a virtual void of opinion on the other.

In the seven weeks studied, the three networks carried seventy-two different stories in which opinion was heard condemning the U.S. policy on the war, and demanding a unilateral bombing halt in opposition to the Johnson policy of reciprocity. Seventy-two stories means that about ten times every week, the networks were pounding America—and the Johnson administration—with opinion opposed to government policies on the war. This editorially selected outcry, subtly interlaced with editorial opinion, came from the following sources: Senators Fulbright, Javits, Morse, and McGovern; Paul O'Dwyer, John Gilligan; Eldridge Cleaver, Dick Gregory, the president of Yale, SDS leader Tom Hayden, actress Vanessa Redgrave; the Socialist Workers' party, the Peace and Freedom party, the Freedom and Peace party, the Socialist Labor party, the Communist party; Arthur Goldberg, George Ball, Averill Harriman, Cyrus Vance; U Thant; Indira Gandhi; Xuan Thuy, the North Vietnamese negotiator; Soviet Premier Kosygin; British and Tokyo demonstrators—and assorted domestic students, demonstrators, black militants, soldiers, pacifists, artists and so on.

Many of these sources were frequently repeated in successive newscasts. It is quite clear that the networks concentrated on the views of an assortment of doves and leftists, foreign and domestic, who were opposed to U.S. war policies.

And what did we hear on the other side? I'll summarize it for you precisely. It was to be found in only thirteen stories—thirteen as opposed to seventy-two, meaning: a six to one ratio against the government:

- ABC aired only four opinions opposed to a unilateral bombing halt in seven weeks—three from President Johnson, alone or in combination with Walt Rostow and Dean Rusk; and one from President Thieu of South Vietnam.
- CBS aired only two such opinions—one from Ohio Republican William Saxbe, and a paraphrased opinion citing "the generals in Vietnam and the secretary of state."
- And NBC also presented two opinions—one from President Thieu, and one from Iowa State Senator David Stanley.

That is: eight opinions in seven weeks opposing a unilateral bombing halt, on all three networks combined.

On the subject of the general war policy:

- ABC aired four favorable opinions—those of President Johnson and Ambassador James Wiggins—twice each.
- CBS aired only one such opinion—from President Johnson.
- And NBC aired none.

That is: five opinions in seven weeks favoring the Johnson policies, on all three networks combined.

This is remarkable coverage indeed of the biggest controversy in the nation. It totally failed to reflect the attitudes in the nation, which at the time was giving President Johnson majority support. The administration's allies, both domestic and foreign, were simply not on the air.

On February 27, 1968, Walter Cronkite presented a special report from Vietnam. In it he said: "It seems now more certain than ever that the bloody experience of Vietnam is to end in a stalement," and he predicted that the United States would not be victorious in this war. And on March 10, 1968, Frank McGee presented a Sunday Report in which he said that "the enemy now has the initiative" and that "the war as the administration has defined it is being lost." The *New York Times* headlines read on March 12: "U. S. is losing war in Vietnam, NBC declares."

Apparently having decided that the war was being lost, these two networks, and ABC as well, resolved to give little or no air time to any view which supported President Johnson's policies.

Whatever one may think about the war, this is not balanced reporting of diverse opinions on a crucial controversy. It is disguised political advocacy.

Very much the same situation prevails in the other controversial areas which I investigated. Over and over again on all three networks—whether the subject was black militants, or the white middle class, or the left, or the right—this lopsided opinion can be found. It favored black power, it opposed the white middle class; it favored the left, it opposed the right. Almost always the opinion was loaded on the left-liberal side of the controversies. Almost always there was a vacuum, or a dramatic shortage, where strong opposition views could and should have been present.

Because of this acute shortage of opinion on one side of almost every controversy, one can state with extraordinary precision which groups in this country were deprived of representation on network news programs during the 1968 period of study. These groups were:

- the broad white middle-class majority, Republican and Democrat
- conservative and Republican leaders
- the broad black majority
- moderate black civil-rights leaders
- and the ideological pro-violence New Left.

And these happen to be the very groups which in 1968 and 1969 charged the networks repeatedly with bias. They, in fact, are exactly what remains when you subtract the left-liberals from the American political spectrum. It is no great surprise that when Vice-President Agnew delivered his speech on network bias a year after the period of this study, there was a volcanic eruption in the nation—with some 57 percent of the public, including 60 percent of all college graduates, supporting him. This public explosion appears to have been a direct and cumulative response to the opinion-loading, to the one-sided advocacy that passed for balanced reporting on controversies.

The Americans who protested are obviously the Americans whose views were chronically left out.

Omission—the crudest slanting technique in the journalistic repertoire—is the principal technique in network slanting. It is perhaps inevitable therefore that when CBS chose to attack *The News Twisters*, its attack was a monument to this very slanting technique.

In September, before *The News Twisters* was published, a ten-page document was distributed to the nation's media by CBS. The mailing literally blanketed the country. It is a study of *The News Twisters* conducted by the CBS News Department itself. It claimed to present hard, documentary evidence of the degree to which I had grossly distorted CBS transcripts. This evidence, said CBS, was based on a "spot check" of those transcripts.

That document is a fraud. Its fraudulence consists in a systematic omission of every conceivable piece of information either from CBS transcripts or from *The News Twisters'* text which would make my classifications intelligible and would reveal the reasoning behind them. The effect of these omissions was to make my work seem arbitrary, irrational and dishonest.

Seventeen charges were listed by CBS—a number that is statistically insignificant for my study, although CBS did not mention that fact to its readers—and of these seventeen charges, fifteen contained active misrepresentations of either CBS transcripts or *The News Twisters'* text or both. I have prepared a detailed report for this Committee in which I identify every misrepresentation; restore every violated context; present the stories that CBS sought to conceal; and I have identified the precise principles by which CBS conducted its so-called random "spot check." My analysis reveals that it was not a "spot check" at all but a carefully calculated smear planned to discredit my book before publication. I call this report "How CBS Tried to Kill A Book." I cannot cite from it; textual analyses must be read. I have given a copy to every member of the Committee and I hope each member will read it. (I have also arranged for copies to be kept on file with this Committee for inspection by the public.) I believe that this report will assist the Committee in its examination of the conflicts that have arisen nationally over network bias.

Now I respectfully submit that the very existence of an ideological oligopoly that controls the airwaves—let alone one which acts to destroy both criticism and critics—is an immense danger to this country. A considerable awareness already exists in Congress of this danger and some substantial proportion of congressmen are as angered by the bias as are members of the public. But Congress is nonetheless afflicted by a characteristic paralysis when it comes to action in this area. Even an explosion of nationwide protest—a protest that included three out of every five college graduates according to the Harris and Gallup polls—could not move Congress into action.

It is quite apparent why the Congress—and the FCC—are paralyzed. This misadventure of Congressman Staggers reveals the bitter truth: that their hands are permanently tied; that they *cannot* act against this monolithic bias on the nation's airwaves; that the Fairness Doctrine is an impotent ideal which cannot be enforced without violation of the First Amendment; that the First Amendment does not deny the right of a news service to be biased, it only states that the news service be free; that even the Supreme Court cannot talk the discrepancy between the Fairness Doctrine and the First Amendment out of existence; and that the nation in fact has no protection whatever from this ideological oligopoly.

The day must come when Congress acknowledges this truth—and more: when it acknowledges that it alone has created this situation, that it is by congressional permission alone that this oligopoly exists and has so long been sheltered from any challenge to its power. On that day, Congress will recognize that this artificial tyranny must be destroyed—by the Congress which brought it into being.

There is only one way to destroy it without violating the First Amendment. That way is not by the petty chivvying and nibbling and the proliferation of regulations that has gone on for years. It is for the government to acknowledge the sacred status of the First Amendment in this country; to acknowledge that it has no business regulating an intellectual and artistic medium—that it never had any business doing so—that it never should have violated the First Amendment rights of individual broadcasters and allowed three nationwide monopolies to form on this intellectually stagnant base—and that it should not year after year, have blocked economic and technological competition in this area to protect the profits of these three giant monopolies.

The government must acknowledge all this however painful it may be. It must get out of broadcasting lock, stock and barrel and let CATV, Pay TV, and cassette technology rip, uncontrolled, unlicensed, unregulated, uncensored, and uninhibited—dominated exclusively by the desire to win voluntary customers, and regulated by the law of supply and demand alone. Only this hurricane of fresh air will bring about in broadcasting the intellectual freedom and diversity that is now lacking.

What is desperately needed in broadcasting is the classical American system that prevails in all the other free media in this land—a free enterprise, *pay* system, in which each producer of intellectual and artistic commodities is absolutely sheltered by the First Amendment; in which each individual consumer purchases only the products that please him and leaves those who have tastes and views alien to his strictly alone. It is this competitive system— free of the twin plagues of government intervention and nationwide monopolistic concentrations of power—which alone has given us the huge spectrum of intellectual and artistic alternatives in this country. It is this proved and honorable system which must be introduced into broadcasting.

Only one thing is needed to accomplish this and that is for government to withdraw from this medium. Poetry does not need the government; plays do not need the government; movies do not need the government; documentaries, newspapers, magazines, novels, photographs and sports events do not need the government. All this country has gotten from government intervention into this realm is the stupidest, most restricted, and most venal medium of communications in the country.

There may be chaos for a while if the government gets out. This chaos would be temporary and supportable. And when it settles, and when the long pent-up creative and competitive energies flow into this government-created vacuum—health will be restored to this medium.

In the process, those arrogant parasitical growths known as the networks will shrink down to the size of normal syndicated operations—selling their wares in an open market and feeling the bite of direct competition for the consumer dollar. This is, of course, precisely as it should be.

The irrational power of the networks today is purely a function of the freedom which has so long been denied to others. It is the government which must take that power back.

Appendix G
Release on INRA Study

... *"The News Twisters"*   March 9, 1972

SECOND INDEPENDENT STUDY REFUTES BIAS CHARGE

An independent study by International Research Associates, Inc. (INRA) has reported findings radically different from the claims made by Edith Efron in her book, *The News Twisters*, after examining transcripts of the same thirty-six "CBS Evening News" broadcasts on which Miss Efron based her charges of news bias.

The study was one of two commissioned by CBS News, the other being an evaluation of Miss Efron's methodology by Dr. Charles Winick, professor of sociology at the City University of New York, completed last Fall.

Using established content analysis techniques accepted by the social science research community, INRA found that while Miss Efron had reported sixteen times greater anti-Nixon material than pro-Nixon material in the thirty-six broadcasts during the 1968 presidential election campaign, the breakdown of all references to the presidential candidates indicated 62 percent of the Nixon material to be neutral, 19 percent judged favorable to him and 19 percent unfavorable.

Where Miss Efron reported that pro-Humphrey material was greater than unfavorable treatment in the same thirty-six broadcasts by a 1.1 to 1 ratio, INRA found a 1.5 to 1 ratio, largely as a result of the way Mr. Humphrey referred to himself. Of the Humphrey material, 57 percent was classified by INRA as neutral, 26 percent as favorable and 17 percent as unfavorable; the differences in the percentage of favorable material (19 percent for Mr. Nixon and 26 percent for Mr. Humphrey) virtually all derived from the different campaign approaches of the two candidates, according to the INRA study. When Mr. Nixon was the sole person talking about himself in the broadcasts, INRA reported, 29 percent of the instances were favorable to him, whereas when Mr. Humphrey was the sole person talking about himself he spoke favorably in his own behalf in 54 percent of the instances. When Mr. Nixon was talking about himself under these same conditions 71 percent of the instances were neutral, whereas in Mr. Humphrey's case the neutral proportion was 43 percent, and 3 percent of the instances were unfavorable to his own cause, as when, according to INRA, he spoke pessimistically about his chances of winning.

INRA analyzed all paragraphs in the transcripts containing references to the presidential candidates not only to determine whether the content was favorable, neutral or unfavorable, but also for the sources of the content, i.e. was it the candidate himself, a CBS newsman or some other source. The study showed that where CBS newsmen were the source, 68 percent of the Nixon material was neutral, 18 percent was favorable to Mr. Nixon and 13 percent was unfavorable, while 66 percent of the Humphrey material was neutral, 18 percent favorable to Mr. Humphrey (the same proportion found for Mr. Nixon) and 16 percent unfavorable, compared to 13 percent unfavorable in the comparable Nixon material.

CBS News also asked INRA to analyze the treatment in the thirty-six broadcasts of ten "issues" included in Miss Efron's book. (The ten "issues" designated in the book are: "U.S. policy on the Vietnam war," "U.S. policy on the bombing halt," "Viet Cong," "black militants," "white middle class," "liberals," "conservatives," "left," "demonstrators" and "violent radicals.") INRA reported that systematic analysis of these "issues" could not be conducted for a number of reasons, principally that they had not been precisely defined and some overlapped (e.g. "liberals" and "left," or "black militants," "demonstrators" and "violent radicals") and also because of the wide-ranging scope of subjects subsumed in some of the "issues" (e.g., Miss Efron's "white middle class" category included "the white middle-class majority," "white America," "white racist America," "the middle-class electorate," "the American electorate" and "the American people"). Consequently, no issue analysis was included in the INRA report.

The full INRA report, as well as the earlier report by Dr. Winick about deficiencies in Miss Efron's methodology, can be obtained from James H. Byrne at CBS News, 524 West 57 Street, New York, New York 10019.

---

[1] This, of course, is contrary to the FCC rule: "The licensee's *overall* performance is considered in determining whether fairness has been achieved on a specific issue. Thus where complaint is made, the licensee is afforded the opportunity to set out *all* the programs, irrespective of the programming format, which he has devoted to the particular controversial issue during the appropriate time period." (Emphasis added.) [1964 *Fairness Primer*, page 1912.]

[2] There is no requirement, under the Fairness Doctrine or otherwise, and it makes no journalistic sense, for a broadcast series, such as the Evening News, to include a mathematically balanced expression of opinions on particular issues. As stated earlier, fairness is determined by an examination of the entire broadcast schedule—not by the limited examination of one broadcast series.